Act Justly, Love Tenderly, Walk Humbly

THIS IS WHAT YAHWEH ASKS OF YOU ONLY THIS

TO ACT
JUSTLY
TO LOVE
TENDERLY
AND
TO WALK
HUMBLY
WITH
YOUR GOD
micah

Act Justly, Love Tenderly, Walk Humbly

Prayers for Peace and Justice

Edward F. Gabriele

Saint Mary's Press
Christian Brothers Publications
Winona, Minnesota

Genuine recycled paper with 10% post-consumer waste.
Printed with soy-based ink.

The scriptural text throughout this book is freely adapted. These
adaptations are not to be interpreted or used as official translations
of the Scriptures.

The publishing team included Carl Koch, FSC, development editor;
Barbara Augustyn Sirovatka, copy editor and typesetter; Lynn Dahdal,
production editor; Sr. Helen David Brancato, illustrator and cover artist;
Stephan Nagel, art director; pre-press, printing, and binding by the
graphics division of Saint Mary's Press.

Printed in the United States of America

Printing: 9 8 7 6 5 4 3 2 1

Year: 2004 03 02 01 00 99 98 97 96 95

ISBN 0-88489-338-3 paper
      0-88489-365-0 spiral-bound

For Oscar Romero and the Slain Women of El Salvador.
For Louis Tesconi and Allen Schindler.
For Victims of Every Human Holocaust
and the Martyred Witnesses who gave their lives for them
out of love for Jesus Christ.
This book is dedicated to their memory
and to the honor of a God
whose Voice speaks "Justice,"
whose Name is "Peace."

Contents

Preface

The official liturgies in the Christian church have been under constant development through the ages. In addition, the history of spirituality gives clear witness to the need for and the presence of evolving forms of personal prayer and time-honored texts for individual devotion; every century has had its texts for personal piety and private devotions. When I wrote *Prayers for Dawn and Dusk* (Saint Mary's Press, 1992), my intention was to publish a four-week cycle of personal prayers drawn from the present Roman Catholic liturgy and other classical forms of Christian worship.

When I finished that first work, something urged me to write other prayer texts out of human experiences. Certainly today the church is more keenly aware of its life and mission within the modern world. In the end, nothing can escape the arena of prayer. No part of our human experience can be hidden from God's gaze. All of life can be brought to fullness in Christ.

This volume contains a four-week cycle of morning and evening prayers written as a springboard for individuals or Christian communities in their ongoing task of learning the language of prayer, a language that arises from experience, is graced and transformed by the power of the Holy Spirit, and then offered back to the world as a gift, bearing the seeds of conversion. These texts were written in the hope that they might help readers develop their own grammar of prayer.

These prayers were completed during the Advent-Christmas season, a season that peaks the imagination and anticipation of believers. However, one disturbing aspect of this time of year is the inevitable and glaring discontinuity between the message of peace that is preached and the realities of social injustice and violence as they are visible to the attentive eye. Amidst

A Theological Reflection

the socializing and pleasures of Christmas, a disturbing presence, a sense of discord can be sensed by attending to the scenes on city streets.

We write cards with festive greetings and wishes for peace, yet we observe the desperate life of poor people whose festivity was robbed years before. We anticipate surprising and thought-filled gifts, yet near and far, some people pass their days waiting to see if the next bomb will destroy their makeshift dwelling. We clink glasses filled with spirits, yet poverty forces many people to grind their teeth on the broken glass of shattered dreams. Folks dance with wild abandon at office parties, yet millions of people stumble to a dirge of disease, addiction, hopelessness, futility, and violence.

With such monumental disparities in our midst, would it not be far easier to forget the poor in our festive oblivion? Why not leave their needs to benefactors, philanthropists, and religious ministers?

Among these bleak reflections, I wonder sometimes if our prayers for justice and peace are not merely mild civilities, nods of acceptable social grace that conveniently absolve our guilt. Why should we pray and work for peace and justice, and what should result from our prayers? Will God avenge the murders of those victimized by death squads? Do we have any hard evidence that God infuses bureaucrats with the will to justice? What could possibly be the result of heart-rending petitions to God for justice, peace, and mercy?

No Cheap Grace

Christian commitment never comes lightly. As Dietrich Bonhoeffer reminded us in his various writings from a Nazi prison before his execution, there is no cheap grace for the believer, no convenient way to believe and worship that can keep God from pushing us back into our world to tend to one another in justice. Pope Paul VI underscored Bonhoeffer's reflections when he said: "If you want peace, then work for justice." Justice must be the essential flower of a personal commitment to the risen Jesus, with peace, the inevitable harvest of that justice, providing the bread of human dignity to all the inhabitants of this world.

In each era, the Christian community has seen the progression of various forms of prayer and spirituality. In our age, we are faced with frightening and unanticipated challenges in world events. Our world stands in desperate need of fresh visions of the Incarnation. If the calls for peace and justice are to be met with responsible prayer and prayerful responsibility in social action, then we must articulate a responsible understanding of the intimate and essential connection between prayer and the needs of social justice and peace in our world.

Earlier in this century when pastoral ministers and theologians argued for the use of the vernacular or local language in the Roman liturgy, far more went on than liturgical window dressing, something deeper and more prophetic. Permitting the language of the people into the official liturgy held theological significance largely unnoticed at that time. Introducing our common languages into the arena of worship brought new dimensions to the church's prayer.

A New Language

Human language is facile, absorbent, adaptive! Confronted with a new phenomena, humans use language as a means of understanding and assimilating what was previously unknown and sometimes frightening. Language can be used as a means of control. In the Scriptures, we find language that may seem strange or even impious. We find real curses that come with blessings. We find men and women of faith using questionable practices, by our standards, to accomplish their interpretation of the will of God. We find the most extraordinary, even criminal, characters chosen as instruments of salvation. Jesus of Nazareth hardly fit the social and religious categories that people anticipated. God will not be limited by our finite logic, our frightened and often rigid imaginations, or our fragile words and utterances. Moreover, the power of God's grace does not wholly depend on our obedience.

Modern media has allowed us to confront or, if we choose, escape the harsh realities of war, disease, famine, oppression, and homelessness. The multiple forms of supportive therapy invite us to explore the darker memories from our psyche. The images of modern Americans leading a controlled and calm lifestyle in middle-class neighborhoods have been abruptly and forever shattered by visions of rape, pillage, terrorism, kidnappings, fraud, and abuse.

Many of our women and children have been abused in horrible ways. We view the bloated bellies of the homeless poor on our city streets or in other lands, and we succumb to the temptation to change the television channel or hurry to our next engagement. We read of the human frailty of civil or religious leaders and wonder if we are humane enough to allow them to be as human, weak, and frail as we are ourselves. Social biases keep the pay and opportunities for women unequal to those of men. The vicious cycle of racial, gender, and ethnic discrimination continues.

Christians must boldly critique their daily activity with the living word of God. The spirit of Christlike conversion should draw us toward renewed and reforming moral activity. So it is essential that the language of social injustice and violence enter into the Christian life of prayer whether communal or personal. A Christian's words of prayer need to be woven together with the cries of poor people, people ravaged by AIDS, unemployed workers, unwelcome refugees, and the victims of new holocausts.

Word Meeting World

The evidence from the Scriptures is clear. Social injustice and violence have always been part of human history. Starting with the murder of Abel, stories of murder, violence, inequality, and injustice fill the Bible. Stories of apathy and collusion with evil appear in both Israel and the early Christian communities. Prophets like Amos screamed for the satisfied rich to share their ill-gotten overabundance with the starving. Jesus fed the poor and consoled the sorrowful while calling hypocritical religious leaders to follow the Law of God more authentically. Paul castigated the Christians of Corinth for daring to commune at the Lord's Supper while discriminating against poor and lowly sisters and brothers, thus fracturing the unity of the Body of Christ.

The Christian tradition calls us to lead just lives and to serve. If we say we love God, then we must love the least of our sisters and brothers because God is truly present among them. Saints like Francis of Assisi and Louise de Marillac have urged us to genuflect before God's presence in poor people much as we bend our knee before the tabernacles within our chapel walls. Our tradition invites the difficulties of life to enter into our prayer, thus renewing us for the hard tasks of doing justice and making peace. The authentic Judeo-Christian tradition calls us to realize the Reign of God now, in our words and actions.

Christianity is a relationship, an intimacy with God, self, others, and the cosmos. Like other human loves and commitments, it invites us to a changed way of living. Believers begin living not for the self but for Christ. Their choices are marked by Christ's truth and a passion for God. Faith in Jesus calls us to prophetic lifestyles, words and actions that witness the real possibilities of just and peaceful living to churches, nations, and neighbors.

Christian prayer arises from the call of God heard within the poor people of our times. In our streets today, the prophet Hosea still speaks to us continually, "Come back to me." Our praying for social justice is vital. Our prayer is a way of bringing all things into the complete arena of our life in Christ. God does not will the subjugation of poor people, the abuse of humans whose full lives are the glory of heaven. God does desire that we take up the struggle of social action.

All of us are called to beat our hatreds into plowshares. Social justice begins as much with the disarmament of the human heart as it does in organizing, demonstrating, or protesting. Prayer helps disarm the human heart. Our prayers heighten both our own and others' awareness. Our prayers for peace and justice strengthen us to be God's instruments. In those prayers, as in all our prayers, liturgical or personal, we remember those in need, we remember our call to serve them, we remember a God who never forgets.

Prayer Disarms the Human Heart

Using the Prayers

The four-week cycle of prayers is divided into the individual phrases from this book's title, phrases that are verses from the prophet Micah: First week, praying to Act Justly; Second week, praying to Love Tenderly; Third week, praying to Walk Humbly. The fourth week is devoted to praise and thanksgiving of the God whose justice and peace are, ultimately, our gifts.

Whether you use the prayers alone or with a group, try to create a prayerful mood with candles, an open Bible, a crucifix, or reminders of particular concerns for justice and peace that are on your mind at the time. If a quiet place is not available, know that a loving God is present everywhere.

The use of first-person plural in the prayers is meant to remind individuals that all our praying takes place as members of the Christian community.

The prayers in this book may be freely adapted to meet your needs. For instance, you may wish to add a hymn at the start or the end of the prayers. Other suggestions follow.

Each hour of prayer is divided into several sections:

- *Presence:* A call to prayer in which the particular intention or image is voiced
- *Prayer:* An original composition that attempts to offer the hour's intention within the wider movements of Christian life and belief
- *Canticle:* Paraphrases from the sacred Scriptures. These draw either from the familiar canticles of the Christian Scriptures or are adaptations of other, more narrative, biblical verses.
- *Silence:* An acknowledgment of the need for reflection and quiet in the course of any prayer
- *Offering:* An invitation, within the spirit of the particular hour of prayer, to offer one's personal needs and intentions
- *The Lord's Prayer:* A recommendation to sum up the hour of prayer with the prayer of Christ. A contemporary adaptation of familiar translations of the Our Father is provided on the inside front cover.

Begin by silently recalling God's presence. If you feel restless or rushed, spend some moments simply relaxing your body, letting go of all the tensions of the day. Breathe deeply and slowly. A period of meditative breathing in God's presence is a prayer of simple attention. If you find it helpful, repeat a short prayer-phrase in harmony with your breathing. For example, "You are present, just and loving God." When you are present to God, engage in the rest of the prayer.

Pray each of the sections carefully, letting the meaning of the words take form for you. Each word and phrase is an offering to God; give your offering deliberately. If a phrase triggers feelings or thoughts that draw you into dialog with God, abandon the printed prayer. Follow your heart and God's promptings. Take time for your own specific intentions and needs.

Thanks

In preparation of this volume, I owe much thanks to Carl Koch, FSC, of Saint Mary's Press, who provided strong enthusiasm and encouragement. Without his initial support and constant editorial leadership, this book would not have been possible. My deep gratitude goes to him and the staff of Saint Mary's Press for their painstaking efforts to hone the final manuscript.

Similar thanks must go to Stephanie Gray, whose personal interest and supportive friendship helped me to develop and bring my words to maturity. The witness of her journey of faith, complete with its joys and pitfalls, gave me good grist for the mill. In addition I am grateful for the afforded time, space, and encouragement of my present colleagues under the leadership of Dr. James Burans, Dr. K. Raviprakash, and Dr. Drew Lewis. Their good-natured curiosity, enthusiasm, special interest, cross-cultural experiences, and particular journeys of spirit, though often not directly articulated, helped sustain me for this work. Deep thanks I must give to another very special colleague, Dr. Mitchell Carl, whose devoted Jewish faith and utterly humane care of his medical patients deepened my own awareness of how much I myself need God to bring me to a deeper peace and justice, a deeper acceptance of myself, in my own daily living.

Finally, I wish to acknowledge several persons from church life whose long-standing Christian witness, scholarship, and faithful friendship led me unknowingly through many years into the writing of this work. Fr. Joseph Serano, fellow theologian and close friend, first introduced me years ago to the prophetic and challenging sociological and theological analyses of Msgr. Paul Hanly Furfey. Furfey's and Serano's thoughts and challenges were present with me constantly as I prepared this text. Also, I must express my gratitude for the social justice witness of Fr. Domenic Rossi and Marie Des Jarlais, FSPA, who left relatively comfortable careers in ministry to risk personal safety and honors for service to the poorest of the poor in this country with the homeless and in Central America with victims of terrorism, respectively. To all of these and the many more who were part and parcel of the long spiritual process that made this volume possible, I give prayerful thanks and appreciation.

Edward F. Gabriele
Feast of the Holy Innocents

First Week
To Act Justly

First Sunday:
For Those in Slavery

MORNING
PRAYER

Presence

Rise up this morning and carry in your heart every person held in slavery. Jesus Christ shall break their chains! At this morning hour, we pray for all those in our world whose lives mirror the image of Jesus bound and scourged at the pillar. We pray for them in hope.

Prayer

God, whose desire is for human freedom,
when your people Israel cried out to you from Egypt,
you saw their tears, stood close to their fears,
and promised them a lasting exodus.
Daylight breaks,
and we are freed from the fears of night.
We bring the living memories to you
of all those who still suffer in slavery.
O God of the dawn, hear the voices of those in chains.
Do not let them live in the shadow of fear,
but tear down their prison walls
and lead them out to the daylight of your liberty.
God of all freedom, never let us grow cold or forgetful.
Overcome our cares and concerns.
Open our ears to hear the cries of those in chains.
Make your mercy bold in us
that your spirit may strengthen us
to be your instruments of justice
until your people are truly set free.
We ask this through Christ and the Holy Spirit,
with you, One God, forever and ever.
Amen.

I will sing to God who is gloriously triumphant,
who has cast horse and rider into the sea.
My strength and my courage is God my savior.
You are my God, and I praise you.
Our enemies boasted: "I will pursue and overtake them;
I will divide the spoils and have my fill of them;
I will draw my sword and my hand shall despoil them."
When your wind blew, the sea covered them;
like lead they sank in the mighty waters.
Who is like you in all creation, O Savior God?
When you stretched out your hand, the earth opened,
and we were saved from our enemies!
In your mercy you led the people you redeemed;
in your strength you guided them to your holy dwelling.
And you brought them in and planted them
on the mountain of your inheritance—
the place you have made your dwelling,
the sanctuary, O God, your hands established.
Our God shall reign forever and ever!

(Exodus 15:1–18)

Silence

Today, O God, we remember the many people in our
world that are held in captivity. We remember their
oppressors as well. Set the captives free, and liberate
their oppressors from the slavery of power. We offer
to you the following special needs . . .

The Lord's Prayer
*(A contemporary adaptation may be found on the inside
front cover.)*

Canticle

Offering

Closing

EVENING PRAYER

Presence

This evening we remember all those held in captivity. Jesus Christ is their pledge of freedom! Darkness is falling upon us, but our hope must never fail.

Prayer

God of all redemption,
this is the day of justice,
the day the captives have been set free.
Jesus, your faithful servant,
you raised up from the power of death
and gave to humanity the hope of freedom.
This night we remember
all those who are yet held in slavery—
those across the seas,
those in our communities,
and those wandering our streets.
May your presence guide us to love and care.
Lead us in deed and word
to proclaim the power of the resurrected Jesus
whose death is our life and whose life is now our hope.
God of every hoping heart,
break the chains that bind us
and teach us to lead one another in justice and peace
until that day when the power of Christ
has moved the spirit of every nation
to set the captives free.
We ask this through Christ and the Holy Spirit,
with you, One God, forever and ever.
Amen.

Praised be God
and our savior Jesus Christ!
Before the world began,
God chose us in Christ
to be holy, free, and blameless.
God predestined us to be adopted through Jesus.
Such was the divine will and pleasure,
that all might praise the glorious favor
that has been bestowed upon us in the Beloved.
Through Christ
we have been redeemed, set free, our sins forgiven.
God has given us the wisdom
to understand the plan carried out in Christ,
    in the fullness of time
to bring all creation to unity and peace,
gathered into the crucified arms of the Beloved
and borne up into the freedom of the ages.

(Ephesians 1:3–10)

Silence

Canticle

God of freedom, the love you plant in us each day
becomes a harvest of liberty through Jesus in the power
of your wisdom. We give you thanks for the ways in
which your freedom has touched us this day, and we ask
especially for the following needs . . .

Offering

The Lord's Prayer

Closing

First Monday: For an End to War

Presence

This day we rise up and bear in mind the fears and
hopes of all those who are threatened by war. Make us
attentive to their needs. We pray for them and hope
that the dawn of peace may come upon them.

Prayer

O God, you created us and formed us in your image.
You are the one God, living and true,
whose desire is for the harmony of all creation.
Even though we disrupted this harmony,
you gave us the promise of peace.
This day we rise from sleep
and hear with our hearts
the din of wartime drums,
the restlessness of human hatred and greed,
the loud anger of friends who have become enemies.
We hear the cries of the victims of war.
We hear the cries of those who defend the poor
       and the weak.
O God, aid us with your gentle strength
to confront all the tyranny
that makes so many hearts beat with fear.
Rid the world of the spirit of aggression
and make our feet dance to the music of peace.
We ask this through Christ and the Holy Spirit,
with you, One God, forever and ever.
Amen.

In future days yet to be revealed,
the house of God
shall be raised up on the highest mountain
for all the nations of the earth to see.
All peoples and races shall run to God's mountain.
They shall stream toward it and say:
"Let us hasten to climb God's mountain.
Let us go up to the God of Jacob and Rachel,
so that we may hear the word of life
and walk in the ways of peace."
For from Mount Zion shall go forth true teaching,
and the word of God will be spoken from Jerusalem.
Only God shall be the lasting judge of the nations.
God shall impose only peace and justice on the peoples.
All human hands shall beat swords into plowshares
and spears into pruning hooks.
One nation shall not raise a weapon against another.
Never again shall the world train for war.
O house of God's faithful, come!
Walk and live in the light of God's peace!

(Isaiah 2:2–5)

Canticle

Silence

Today, O God, we remember the many places in the
world that are threatened by the horrors of war and
human hatred. We remember those who can lead the
nations to peace and justice. We offer to you the
following special needs . . .

Offering

The Lord's Prayer

Closing

EVENING
PRAYER

Presence

This evening we remember the people of the world
who hunger and thirst for peace, and the peacemakers
who build harmony and right relationships. We pray for
them in the hope of lasting peace and justice.

Prayer

God of peace,
you created us in freedom
and gave us the whole world
to steward in your love.
In the fullness of time, we formed ourselves
        into nations,
and quickly gave way to the temptations
of power, greed, and injustice.
To satisfy the corrupt urgings of our hearts,
we took up arms
and planted fear where you desired peace.
In the fullness of time, you sent to us
        your incarnate Word
who called us back to the full awareness
        of your loving care.
This Jesus breathed the spirit of peace upon the world,
healed our wounds, suffered with us,
and raised us to hope.
This night and forever,
banish from our lives the will to make war.
Put an end to those fears
that urge nations to do battle.
Never again may we raise a hand against another.
Never again may we mar the beauty of this world
        with war.
We ask this through Christ and the Holy Spirit,
with you, One God, forever and ever.
Amen.

We praise you, God, the mighty and gentle,
you, the eternal God of peace!
You are ageless power
and reign with infinite justice!
The nations have raged in battle.
But then came your day of justice,
the moment to judge the living and the dead,
the time to reward your servants,
the holy ones who revere you,
the great and the lowly alike.
Now have salvation and true power come,
the Reign of our God
and the gentle authority of the Anointed One.
For the accusers and warmongers of the world
have been exposed for their sinfulness,
the evil ones whose whispers of greed and hatred
brought the innocent to war.
The Prince of Peace has empowered the powerless
and replaced the spirit of war
with the desire for peace.
Love for life did not deter them
from offering their lives to protect the lowly.
So rejoice, heaven and earth,
and all those who hope for peace!

(Revelation 11,12)

Silence

God of peace, we are mindful that war begins with hate, not weapons. We are grateful that you teach us to travel on paths other than the way of violence. We are mindful of those who work for the cause of peace and grateful for their witness of gentle compassion. We pray especially for the following needs . . .

The Lord's Prayer

Canticle

Offering

Closing

First Tuesday:
For an End to Famine

Presence

We rise from sleep, attentive to the voices of all those who hunger for bread and thirst for dignity. God alone provides the bounty of food to all living things, but we are God's stewards. Together with the servants of God in every age, we remember all those who suffer from hunger.

Prayer

God of every gift,
you created in us
the need for food and drink
and asked us only for our gratitude in return.
We tilled the soil and tended the vines,
kneaded bread and provided drink
to satisfy our human hungers.
But in every age, greed and envy
led us to forget your loving graces
that called us to share our goods
with those who are less fortunate.
So you sent prophets to speak your word
and to call us to feed the hungry.
Jesus, your beloved child, fed the masses,
and, on that final night, took bread and cup
and fed us with the presence of all life itself.
Rouse up the spirit of your love.
Teach us again to feed the poor.
Strengthen us to share our bread with all the hungry.
We ask this through Christ and the Holy Spirit,
with you, One God, forever and ever.
Amen.

All you nations of the earth,
hear the word of life, the word of God,
proclaim it in distant lands and say:
"The God who scattered the tribes of Israel,
now gathers them together,
guarding them as a shepherd tenderly guards a flock."
The gentle God shall ransom Israel,
redeeming the people from the hand of conquerors.
Shouting, the nation shall mount the heights of Zion,
streaming to the bounty of the reign of heaven:
the grain, the wine, the oil,
the sheep, and the oxen;
the people shall be like a watered and tended garden,
never again shall they languish in hunger and thirst.
Then young women shall lead the dance
and take the men by the hand.
They shall lead the elders and the young ones
    in festivity.
I, the God of the harvest, shall turn their hungers
    into feasting,
their mourning into joy.
I will console and gladden them after their sorrows
    and famine.
I will lavish them with the choicest of foods
and fill my people with all blessings,
says the God of feasting.

                (Jeremiah 31:10–14)

Silence

Canticle

Today, bountiful God, we remember the poor of this world who struggle to feed themselves and their children. We remember those who hunger for justice and peace. We offer to you the following special needs . . .

Offering

The Lord's Prayer

Closing

EVENING PRAYER

Presence

As evening draws near, our hearts hear the cries of those whose work does not earn sufficient food and drink. We listen to the suffering of those whose bellies are bloated by famine. In prayer, we join their voices to our own as we call upon the God of bounty.

Prayer

God of the harvest,
you do not desire your people to suffer.
Rather, you look to have us love one another
and give to each other the goodness of food and drink.
Jesus, your beloved,
did not shrink from the poor and the hungry,
but satisfied those who starved for bread
        and human dignity.
In every age, your spirit of love calls us
to attend to your very presence
in the poor and the starving among us.
Breathe forth that spirit among us.
Put to flight the powers of greed and selfishness.
Break into the shadows of our lives
and enlighten us to new ways of selfless love.
Teach all the nations of the earth
to tend the soil for a new bounty
that will feed the hungry with bread and justice.
We ask this through Christ and the Holy Spirit,
with you, One God, forever and ever.
Amen.

All praise to God!
Salvation, glory, honor, and power
belong to the God who feeds all living things.
The justice of God fills up all that we lack.
All praise to God!
Sing praise to our God, all servants of mercy.
The lowly and the proud, the hungry
 and those who have their fill,
worship our God with reverence.
All praise to God!
This is our God, the mighty of heaven and earth,
the gentle companion who leads us on our pilgrim way.
Rejoice, sing praise and give God glory.
All praise to God!
Now has the wedding feast of the Lamb begun.
The hungry are filled with all good things.
The lowly are rescued from despair.

(Revelation 19:1–7)

Silence

God of every good thing, this night we remember your
command that we must love one another. Conscious
that your love calls us to feed the hungry, hear our
prayers for those who suffer from famine, and especially
for the following needs . . .

The Lord's Prayer

Canticle

Offering

Closing

First Wednesday:
For an End to Poverty

Presence

The sun rises, and we wake from sleep. Heighten our
awareness of the poor and the homeless in our midst,
their silent needs, like the voice of Christ, asking us
to clothe and feed them.

Prayer

O God, you are the defender of the poor
and the stronghold of the orphaned and the widowed.
When your people were robbed of their homes
and put into chains,
you did not abandon them
but made of them a special people.
From the remnants of their lives
you fashioned them into a garment of joy.
In the fullness of time, you sent Christ
who announced the good news of salvation to the poor,
the day of liberty for those in need.
In these days, the nightmare of poverty
haunts our world and enters our homes.
Standing in lines, deprived of human dignity,
the poor of our world beg for our love
and ask for food and work.
Shine your spirit of courage and compassion upon us.
Warm the cold of our hearts and wills.
Help us to help your beloved poor.
Help us to see that in loving and tending their needs
we are tending the presence of Christ among us.
We ask this through Christ and the Holy Spirit,
with you, One God, forever and ever.
Amen.

My heart exults in the living God,
I rejoice in the One who loves me.
I have conquered my oppressors.
I rejoice in the victory God has put before me.
There is no holy one like this God.
There is no rock like Yahweh.
The bows of the mighty and the arrogant wealthy
    are broken,
while the weak and the feeble are given strong limbs.
The well-fed haughty ones must hire themselves out
while the humble hungry feast on fine food.
God puts to death and gives life,
casting down to the nether world
    and raising us up again.
Yahweh makes poor and makes rich,
humbling and exalting beyond our dreaming.
God raises the needy from the dust,
from the ashes the poor are lifted
to take their places in our midst
and to make glory their heritage!
For not by the strength of mere human means
    do we survive,
but by the strength of God
who has exalted the Anointed One!

(1 Samuel 2:1–10)

Silence

Canticle

Today, O God, you bring before us the poor and home-less. As this new day breaks upon us, we are called to serve them as we would ourselves. We offer to you these special needs . . .

Offering

The Lord's Prayer

Closing

EVENING PRAYER

Presence

Our day is drawing to a close, yet our mind, though needing rest, still gathers in the images of those whose needs for daily living have gone unfulfilled. This night, the poor and those without a place to lay their head are present to us, asking us to remember them and to care for their needs in love.

Prayer

O God of every gift,
you do not desire the suffering of any of your creatures.
From the beginning, you called us to care
       for one another.
Yet in every age,
nations have let the poor wander through the streets
robbed of hope, bellies empty, and hearts broken.
This night we remember
that you sent your beloved Jesus into our world,
to share in the common life
of those who were downtrodden and deprived.
By choice, Jesus had no place to lay his tired head.
Yet from daylight to day's end,
he walked and ate with the poor and homeless
       of his age.
Jesus loved them and fed their needs,
and called all disciples to do the same.
This night send forth your light into our lives
and scatter our insensitivity and fear.
Move our sluggish hearts to aid the poor
and to help the homeless find safe shelter.
We ask this through Christ and the Holy Spirit,
with you, One God, forever and ever.
Amen.

Christ suffered at the hands of the mighty.
He left us an example of selfless love
so that we might follow in the footsteps of salvation.
In that blameless life,
there was no wrongdoing,
no malice of any kind.
Jesus spoke the healing and prophetic truth.
He was insulted,
but returned no insult,
no rage, no anger, or resentment.
Suffering at the hands of soldiers and powers,
Jesus did not counter them with threats
or promises of retribution.
Instead, to embrace our fears and our dying,
Jesus held his hands out
and was led to the place of crucifixion.
Indeed, Christ was delivered
into the hands of the One who alone judges justly.
In his body, Jesus brought our poverty to the cross,
so that all of us, dead to sin,
could live alone for God.
In these wounds, we have been healed.

(1 Peter 2:21–24)

Silence

Canticle

God of the poor and the homeless, Jesus abandoned himself into your hands upon the cross. This night we remember the needs of the poor and the homeless. We bring them before you, and we remember the following special needs from our heart . . .

Offering

The Lord's Prayer

Closing

First Thursday:
For the Sick and Dying

Presence

As this new day begins, the God of our longing is
present to us in those among us who are sick and dying.
Conscious that their image reflects our own limitations
and frailties, we carry them in prayer this day. Our
remembrance is for them a light of strength in their
suffering, a hope of redemption, and a consolation
as they go on their journey.

Prayer

O God, you are the hope of all who suffer.
Sometimes we may seek to ignore
the sufferings of the sick, the limits of the human body,
and the inevitability of human death.
But through the grace of memory,
we are not capable of completely banishing
	the presence of disease
or the fear of dying that walks with us through life.
You yourself did not shrink from sharing
	in these painful moments.
Jesus, your beloved, touched the sick,
shared the sorrows of those who mourned,
and, on that final Friday, stretched out his arms
and brought into your divine embrace
	the full fear of death.
Your presence to those who are sick and dying
is a consolation and a strength
as they go on a journey
	from which they cannot turn aside.
Give us the strength to do the same for them.
Be present to those who serve their needs
	at bedside and in hospice.
Do not let us run in terror.
Rather, let us be your reassuring presence.
We ask this through Christ and the Holy Spirit,
with you, One God, forever and ever.
Amen.

Once I said:
"At the very height of my life I must leave this world
and pass through death to an eternity I do not know.
No longer shall I know the joy of beholding
my sisters and brothers in this world."
My earthly home, like a tent,
is struck and taken away from me.
Like a spider's web or fine silk threads,
my life is cut sharply and abruptly off
and whisked away.
Day and night I am given over to fear and suffering.
I cry in terror until the break of day.
My sickness is a torment, an agony.
O God, preserve me!
Indeed, O God, you save my life from final doom
when you blot out the memory of my sins.
There is no praise for you in eternal death.
Fully living gives you glory.
May my hope of your salvation be fulfilled
and become the glad song of victory.

(Isaiah 38:10–14,17–20)

Silence

At this beginning of a new day, we place before God
the needs of suffering and dying people. God, ever
present to us in our every need, we offer our prayers for
all who suffer, especially these special needs . . .

The Lord's Prayer

Canticle

Offering

Closing

EVENING PRAYER

Presence

The shadows of night are falling upon us quickly, and they bring to mind those whose suffering darkens their hope and understanding. Let us be present to the needs of the sick and the dying as we bring their presence before the God of hope and consolation.

Prayer

O God, your ways are beyond our comprehension.
The design and rhythms of life and death
are not at the commands of our words or hands.
Knowing that sickness and death come for us all,
we run to stem the tide of our growing older.
The limits of this life strike us fully in the face:
news of the young who die suddenly,
the despairing who take their lives,
the new lepers abandoned unjustly,
the dead whom no one will mourn.
How do we give you praise
    when there seems to be no peace
in the tragic news that fills our homes
and pierces our hearts with grief and fear?
Yet you dwell among us.
Jesus holds us with your tenderness
and bids us do the same for one another.
Stir up the spirit of strength and hope.
Make us strong enough
to enter the vulnerability of the sick and dying.
Help us to accompany them on their journey
until at last we come to your peace
where every tear will be wiped away,
every fear replaced by glory.
We ask this through Christ and the Holy Spirit,
with you, One God, forever and ever.
Amen.

Eternal God,
you alone are worthy
to receive the full adoration of all the peoples
  of the earth.
You are the one who brought to life
every rock and tree,
every planet and star,
every woman and man.
You breathed,
and life itself was brought to birth!
Worthy are you, O God,
to receive the scroll of life and break open its seals.
For in your Lamb, you tasted our human dying.
Through Jesus were ransomed
people of every race and color and tongue.
You made of them one people,
ordained them to give you fitting praise,
and they shall tend the world in holiness and joy.
Worthy is this Lamb, the one who suffered with us.
Worthy is the Lamb, the innocent victim
who has ransomed us from a final dying.
Worthy is the Lamb, whose wisdom and strength
guard our nights and days into eternity!
     (Revelation 4:11; 5:9,10,12)

Silence

Loving God, in a special way our sick and dying sisters
and brothers reflect the image of Christ among us. Do
not let us grow cold to their needs. Hear our prayers for
them at this evening hour. We bring them to you
as we offer our special intentions . . .

The Lord's Prayer

Canticle

Offering

Closing

First Friday: For Conversion of the Nations

Presence

The morning has dawned, and we are called to hold the needs of the nations before you. You, God, call every people to charity and justice. May we embrace your wisdom: "Harden not your hearts." As the day begins, we remember our common call to conversion of life and sincerity of heart.

Prayer

O blessed Creator,
you fashioned women and men to give you praise.
From the unity of your love,
our world has seen the progress of many peoples,
the birth of many nations,
the art and science in many languages.
Yet too often, the human spirit has been lured
by selfish greed,
the arrogance of warlike pride,
and the lust of pride and power.
Into a nation shackled by oppressors,
Jesus was born and lived in gentleness of spirit.
Maligned for the miracles of compassion
and for the truth he preached,
condemned as dangerous to the people,
Jesus was delivered into the hands of those fearful
of his healing, his love, and his truth.
Send forth the power of your Holy Spirit.
Convert the nations to your love.
Inspire us to put away hatred
and set your people free.
We ask this through Christ and the Holy Spirit,
with you, One God, forever and ever.
Amen.

Blessed be the God who lives forever and ever!
The Reign of God's justice and peace is eternal,
never marred by human pride.
God purifies us, but always with mercy.
Those thrown down into the depths
are raised from the pit of despair.
No nation can escape the power of Yahweh.
Praise God, you Israelites, from among the nations.
Though you were scattered among foreign lands,
God has brought you mercifully home.
Exalt God before everything that lives and breathes
because this God, like a mother and father,
leads and nourishes you to fullness of life.
Indeed, you suffered for your iniquities.
From suffering you learned not to shrink
        from God's will.
No longer does God hide from your needs.
From the land of exile you were brought forth
with ancient words of wisdom: "Turn back,
        you sinners."
Let all peoples speak of the mercy of God,
a mercy that turns back the nations from sin.

(Tobit 13:1–8)

Canticle

Silence

As daylight breaks, we gather our needs before you,
God of compassion. We pray this day for every nation
and people that mercy may be the hallmark of governments and cultures. For the progress of true justice
among all people we offer our special needs . . .

Offering

The Lord's Prayer

Closing

EVENING
PRAYER

Presence

Now evening stretches across us. The mercy of God,
like a lamp in the darkness, enlightens our ways and
guides us through the terror of night. So we pray for the
conversion of the nations and that all people may know
just governments and peaceful lives.

Prayer

O God,
you are the foundation of every righteous nation.
At the Tower of Babel,
prideful people built an arrogant humanity
that ended, predictably, in destructive confusion.
But Jesus called forth a new nation,
a people of justice and peace,
     a race peculiarly your own.
In a dim upper room, your Holy Spirit
     made courageous witnesses
of those who were shadowed by lost hopes
and the fear of their own persecution for the Word.
From that room, the new Law of Love
was spoken to a hungry world
whose nations are starving still
     from oppression and violence.
This night and forever, make your Spirit burn brightly
     in our midst.
Rid every government of the will to wage war
and the desire to oppress.
Raise up leaders for your people
whose words will inspire us to new deeds of compassion.
Bring all the world to conversion of life
that your justice might be a light for our paths.
We ask this through Christ and the Holy Spirit,
with you, One God, forever and ever.
Amen.

Though made in the fullness of God,
Jesus did not deem equality with God
something to cling to.
Rather, Christ took our human flesh,
being born in our very likeness.
Jesus was fully human.
Christ was humbled,
obediently accepting human death,
death like a common criminal.
But because of this,
God raised Jesus from the pit of death
to the heights of glory.
God gave to Jesus a name
above all other names and powers.
So at the very mention of the name of Jesus
every knee, every power, every nation should bow:
everything that lives in the heavens,
on the earth and under the earth.
And every tongue and race and people should proclaim,
to the glory of the mighty and gentle God,
that Jesus is the Christ,
the anointed savior of the nations.

(Philippians 2:6–11)

Silence

Living God, this night we remember our common call
to conversion, a call shared by all the nations of the
earth. Conscious of our need to turn back to you at
every moment of our life, we offer you our prayers for
the conversion of the nations. Consider these special
prayers . . .

The Lord's Prayer

Canticle

Offering

Closing

First Saturday:
For an End to Discrimination

Presence

As morning comes and sunlight binds us together in
the new day, we are called to tear down the walls of
discrimination and make new progress in the unity of
our human family. We pray this day for the grace to
love courageously beyond our human fears and doubts.

Prayer

O God, you fashioned our human family in love
and called us from the beginning
to join our hearts and hands as one people
to proclaim your truth and tend the gifts of all creation.
But from the distrust born of our first parents
and the innocent blood of Abel spilled
    out of jealous rage,
we turned aside from the path of unity
and made enemies where only friends
were meant to be found.
This day we repent of the ways we have invented
to tear our hearts from one another
    in oppression and hatred.
We have not welcomed the stranger and the orphan.
We have oppressed each other by sinful spite
and given free reign to the evil of prejudice.
This day let your light melt the ice of our human hating.
Let the voice of Jesus in our midst call us
    to build a new order
in which people of every race,
of every language and persuasion
can live together in peace.
We ask this through Christ and the Holy Spirit,
with you, One God, forever and ever.
Amen.

Truly within your midst God is hidden,
the God of Israel, the God of all creation,
the God of every race and people and nation.
This is no God who makes distinctions,
who allows the shame of the human heart
to judge the worthiness of flesh and blood
by the color of the skin
or the thoughts one thinks in secret.
Israel, you are saved by Yahweh.
Never again shall you be shamed before the world.
Thus says Yahweh: "I am your God, yours alone.
I have not spoken my word in hiding.
I have spoken my word before all creation
to bind you as one people
living in my promise of justice,
    my dreaming of your peace."
Come before God with joy.
Do not wander in the wasteland of your senseless fears.
Do not worship the idols of oppression.
Turn to God and be safe.
Offer the safety of Yahweh to every people.
Only in God can be found just deeds
    and the power of loving.
For in God alone shall be the end of all fears
and the glory of every human heart.

(Isaiah 45:15–25)

Canticle

Silence

On this day, we remember the many ways that we have
discriminated against so many people. We confess our
need to turn away from the sin of our prejudice, to turn
toward the God of all people. This day we pray for
those who have suffered oppression, especially for . . .

Offering

The Lord's Prayer

Closing

EVENING PRAYER

Presence

Night is falling, and we are mindful of the many bleak hours that fall upon those who are the innocent victims of human prejudice and discrimination. This night we bear them up to the light of Jesus Christ, whose justice and grace can heal their wounds and call their oppressors to conversion.

Prayer

O God, you are the source of every human life,
the healer of every wound,
and the voice that calls our loving to deeper places.
This night we remember and confess
the many ways that we have oppressed the poor
and caused fear to reign in our midst
by the tragedy of unjust discrimination.
In you there are no distinctions,
no features of our bodies, souls, minds, or spirits
that could cause you to turn away from us.
We are your children, your cocreators.
And you love us as you love yourself.
Yet despite the word of Jesus,
        we still do not love one another
with the same equality and care you show us all.
Let the power of your Spirit be a bright fire in our midst.
Burn up the fears that make us senseless
and cause us to maim our freedom
        by the horrors of prejudice.
Do not let us turn our backs upon each other.
Teach us to do what Jesus did,
embracing our diversity as the foundation of our unity.
We ask this through Christ and the Holy Spirit,
with you, One God, forever and ever.
Amen.

Now let me teach you of the greatest gift,
the richness of God that is deeper than all else.
If I were to speak the language of the angels
and absorb all the learning of the world
yet live without an embracing love,
my presence would be as lasting
as the passing notes
of brass chimes sounding briefly in the wind.
If I were to have all the gifts
that human foolishness counts as great
yet not have love,
I would have no greatness at all.
Love is patient. Love is kind.
Love does not seek its own reward.
Love does not breed hatred and prejudice and fear.
Love is without limits or discriminations.
Love never fails.
All else will indeed come to an end.
But love will never cease.
There are in God's eyes three things that last:
faith, hope, and love.
And the greatest of these is love!

(1 Corinthians 13)

Silence

God of justice and peace, this night we bring before you
the tragedies of prejudice and discrimination that we
have built up in our human family. We pray for an end
to these evils, and we pray for those who have been
victimized by our fears. We pray for those who feed
upon our nightmares, and we offer these special needs
to you . . .

The Lord's Prayer

Canticle

Offering

Closing

Second Week
To Love Tenderly

Second Sunday:
For Love Among Christians

MORNING PRAYER

Presence

On this day of Christ's victory, we remember Jesus' invitation to love one another and to create community. We bring to the light of this new day the needs of the people of God, the community of love in Christ Jesus.

Prayer

O God, from the dawn of creation
you formed a people to be your own.
In every age, the gentle call of your voice
gathers diverse believers
to form one people to give you praise.
Today we remember that Jesus,
God-with-us, created a new people,
the communion of hearts
we have called church.
Hardly perfect in our life together,
we often forget the command of Christ
to love one another without discrimination
and to be witnesses of love to every race and nation.
By the strong power of your Spirit
bind us in compassion for each other.
Teach us again the meaning of your love
that we may proclaim to every age
the salvation of the whole world in Christ.
We ask this through Christ and the Holy Spirit,
with you, One God, forever and ever.
Amen.

Behold! New days are coming!
I will make a new covenant
with the houses of Israel and Judah.
I will bind myself anew with my people.
It will not be like that first covenant,
the one I made in ancient times
when I took you by the hand
and led you out from Egypt's slavery.
This time I will place my word within you,
my law will be written in your hearts.
I will be your only God;
you shall be my people.
No longer will you need a teacher.
No longer shall you stray from my loving.
Your lives will instruct all people.
All races and tongues, the small and the great,
shall know my presence in your midst.
I will forgive your sins.
I will blot out your transgressions
and remember your sinful ways no more.
Yes, I am your God.
You are my people.

(Jeremiah 31:31–34)

Silence

As day shines upon us, we remember that God's love
has filled our life through Christ. This day we remember the needs of God's people, the church throughout
the world. For an increase of God's love in our midst,
we offer now our special needs . . .

The Lord's Prayer

Canticle

Offering

Closing

EVENING PRAYER

Presence

Day is coming to a close. Yet even with the nighttime our hopes never grow dim, for the light of Jesus leads us toward a new day of justice, love, and peace. Tonight we remember our call to unity as the people of God. We hold up to the mighty and gentle One our need to be graced with strength so that we might love one another and proclaim the joy of the Resurrection to all humanity.

Prayer

God ever-present,
on this night Jesus came to those first friends
and breathed on them a peace
that is beyond all understanding.
Peace sounds simple,
yet living in peace and love escapes us.
As your holy people, your church,
you have called us to speak words of peace
and to live together in charity.
This night we confess
that our human weaknesses
have kept us from loving each other
as Christ has loved us.
Remove from our hearts our fear of loving,
our pride and sinful greed.
Make us hunger for each other's friendship.
Help us to remember that apart from your loving
we have no life.
We ask this through Christ and the Holy Spirit,
with you, One God, forever and ever.
Amen.

I am the vine
and you are the branches of my love.
The Creator is the vine dresser
who prunes away every barren branch
that grows up in your life.
The fruitful are trimmed clean
so that their yield of love will increase and grow.
You have been pruned and cleaned already.
My word has trimmed your life
and made you fruitful.
Live in my love.
For I live in you each moment.
No branch can ever survive
when it is cut away from the vine and its roots.
No fruit can grow from barren branches.
Nor can you live or grow
apart from my loving presence in your midst.
Apart from my love,
you cannot bear fruit.
Remain in my life always
and feed the nations with my loving.

(John 15:1–4)

Silence

God of all love, tonight we are grateful that you have
bound us together as one people in the love of Jesus
Christ. We bring to you the needs of your people,
especially our need for an increase of love for one
another. In this spirit, we remember these special
intentions . . .

The Lord's Prayer

Canticle

Offering

Closing

Second Monday:
For the Harmony
of All Nations

Presence

As a new day begins, we are mindful of the need for harmony among all the nations of the world. We bring before you, gracious God, the need for world peace and for governments to establish justice for every woman, man, and child.

Prayer

O God, you are the foundation of peace
among every race and people,
among every city, village, and tribe.
From the dawn of creation,
we have been gathered as a family of nations
whose gifts of culture and progress
are born from the goodness of your love.
But in the course of the centuries,
rulers and powers have raged against each other.
Greed and power
have clouded the vision of your dignity
that is our rightful heritage.
Break the chains of prejudice and hatred among us.
Teach us to put aside war and injustice.
Draw us to live in peace and harmony.
Jesus showed us how to hope and how to heal;
may we learn from him.
We ask this through Christ and the Holy Spirit,
with you, One God, forever and ever.
Amen.

See! I am about to make a new nation
of the house of Jacob and Rachel.
I am about to restore the tents of Israel
and make of them a dwelling of my compassion!
Cities shall be rebuilt upon the heights of love,
and palaces will no longer be arrayed
    with warlike power.
From every mouth shall go forth
songs of praise and the laughter of hearts made happy.
I will take my remnant and make them fruitful.
I will make many people where there were only few.
I will take the small and make them great.
I will take the children and make them prosper.
I will rid the land of all oppressors
and banish the forces of evil and hatred.
I will raise up a leader fashioned after my own heart
and rid my people of every tyrant.
I will bring my people before me
in freedom and holiness of life.
You shall be my people,
my sign of justice for all creation.
I shall be your only God,
your savior, and your love.

(Jeremiah 30:18–22)

Silence

Canticle

This day we remember that God has fashioned us as
many cultures and many people, each singing praise in
varied, lively ways. We pray for harmony among
nations. We offer the needs of world peace to God, and
we remember these special intentions . . .

Offering

The Lord's Prayer

Closing

**EVENING
PRAYER**

Presence

As this day draws to a close, the spirit of God keeps us mindful of the needs of every nation, the need of every people for harmony, justice, and peace. This night we bear the presence of every nation before the God whose love alone renews the human heart.

Prayer

God of every nation,
this night we recall your many gifts to us
in language and culture and history.
At the foot of the cross,
Jesus gathered the family of nations
to bathe us in that life-giving salvation
that alone is our hope of peace and justice.
Look upon each city and people,
see us even in our selfish ways.
Help us banish from our life
greed and lust for power.
Teach us to steward all of creation
and to make our life conform
to the selfless harmony of your heart.
Lead us away from oppression and warlike ways.
Show us how to honor differences
among all the varied cultures that compose
    the human family.
Help us to see in each other
the multitude of ways you love us.
We ask this through Christ and the Holy Spirit,
with you, One God, forever and ever.
Amen.

I am the true vine.
You are the branches.
If you only would find your life in me
and let me live fully in your life as well,
then you would bear the fruit of justice
and have an abundance of life forever.
Apart from the life that is mine,
you can have no life;
you cannot bear the fruit of peaceful ways.
If any of you refuse to live in me,
then you will die hopelessly like a withered branch.
Those who are cut off from my love
can know nothing but the brush pile.
If you live in me and let my life well up within you,
you may ask the Creator for anything,
nothing good will be refused to you.
Whenever you live in my love,
and bear the fruit of heaven to all peoples,
then you give glory to God,
the Creator of all living things.

(John 15:5–8)

Silence

God of every human longing, the people cry out for the
gift of your lasting peace. Though we have often stirred
up disharmony, your grace can bring us back. This
night we raise up to you our need to be renewed in your
love. We bring every nation before you, and we remember these special intentions . . .

Offering

The Lord's Prayer

Closing

Second Tuesday: For Love in Every Family

Presence

A new day has come upon us with new graces and new invitations to God's love. Today we remember every human family and every gathering of human hearts in peace and justice. We bring before God all those who hunger and thirst for the warmth of human loving.

Prayer

O God, you are the root of every family tree.
In the beginning, you planted in our hearts and bodies
the desire for unity
and the strong hope of loving
that dispels our fears and despair.
Now we recall the many gatherings of faith and love
that are our families.
We remember the visions and dreams of love
that have drawn adults and children
to live in homes of peace and joy.
Yet we are also mindful
of those whose lives have been scarred
by selfishness and abuse.
We bring to you hearts harmed by vengeful words
and by hands raised in cruelty and rage.
Look upon our homes and families.
Calm our fears.
Build up every human home in peace
and make each family to be your dwelling
and the place of your glory.
We ask this through Christ and the Holy Spirit,
with you, One God, forever and ever.
Amen.

Shout with joy for Rachel and Jacob
exult for good parents.
Proclaim to every human gathering:
"God has delivered all the people,
God has brought salvation to the remnant of Israel."
Behold! I will bring you back
from the land of your sorrow and exile.
I will gather you as one family
from all the nations of the earth.
I will bear upon my shoulders
the blind and the lame,
those with children and those without.
I will bring you back as my people
who dance before me with song and shouts.
Those who are sorrowing, I make laugh.
Like a mother, I will bring you to birth.
Like a father, I will tend your needs.
Like children, I will give you delight.
For you are my children, my people.
And I am your God!

(Jeremiah 31:7–9)

Silence

At this morning hour, we remember women and men
and children. We remember all those who gather
themselves under the name *family.* We bring to you,
God, their many needs for love and harmony and
healing. With them, we offer these special intentions
to you who hears our prayers . . .

The Lord's Prayer

Canticle

Offering

Closing

**EVENING
PRAYER**

Presence

This day has come to a close, and we are gathered from our many labors into homes that are continually in need of being built up in the love of Christ. Jesus is our hope for the coming of a time when all of us will be comforted by tender, caring love.

Prayer

God of tender love,
as evening falls upon us,
we are mindful that you give families the gift of love.
Whether newly born or advanced in age,
your people have celebrated your gift of human passion
by gracing each other with faithful care.
Yet ignorance, anger, and selfishness
so often rip this loving apart.
Sin and affliction
can blind our souls to your graces
brought to birth in our midst.
By the power of your Holy Spirit,
take away all that would divide our families
and place within our hearts
a hunger and thirst for your goodness.
Let every family bear your name in their home.
Let your love be seen among us.
We ask this through Christ and the Holy Spirit,
with you, One God, forever and ever.
Amen.

As God has loved me tenderly
so I love you as well.
If you would be drawn into our life,
then live forever in our loving.
This love you keep and tend
when you embrace my commandments,
commandments I have kept
as God has whispered them to me.
All these things I tell you
to give you the gift of joy,
the pure joy that comes your way
from my life and from my God.
This alone is your one commandment,
the one law for you to live:
Love one another deeply,
as I have loved you.
Bear no evil against each other.
Do not bruise or harm or hurt.
Live in the love that I have poured out upon you.
Love one another
as I have loved you all.

(John 15:9–12)

Silence

God of love, every human family draws its life from
your heart. There can be no life where your love is not
present. This night we bring before you the needs of
our families. Asking for an increase of your love in their
midst, we bring you these special intentions . . .

The Lord's Prayer

Canticle

Offering

Closing

Second Wednesday: For the Gift of Loving Friends

Presence

Night is over, and day has dawned. With this new day,
we are called to prayer. Our God has given us Jesus as
the true friend who is our constant companion on this
earthly pilgrimage. We remember all those who are our
friends, and we pray for an increase of true friendship in
our life.

Prayer

O God, when you created our human family,
you did not desire that we should live in loneliness
or never know love.
In time, we learned to join our hands and heart
with other men and women
whose warmth and tenderness
invited us to call them friends.
This day, drawn from the many corners of life,
whether from solitude
or the hurry of the workplace,
we remember our need for human loving
that inspires us to leave our fears behind
and make new friends of strangers.
You have given us your beloved Jesus
to strengthen us in human friendship.
With the presence of Christ among us,
teach us to put aside our fear of being loved
and help us to give and take the gift of friendship
to those we meet this day.
We ask this through Christ and the Holy Spirit,
with you, One God, forever and ever.
Amen.

On the day of my justice and peace,
I will gather every human heart.
I will gather up the lame and all the sick.
I will gather in the outcasts and the oppressed.
I will take away affliction and sorrow.
I will wipe away every tear and bitterness.
I will make lame ones dance.
I will make a strong nation of those who are weak.
I will open my arms in friendship
to those who have suffered and despaired.
I will be the Shepherd-Ruler
whose love flows from Mount Zion.
And you, city of Jerusalem,
capital of my faithful people,
you are the eldest of my child, Zion.
Your dishonor shall be blotted out and taken away.
Your suffering and loneliness shall come to an end.
To you I will bring the delight of my justice.
My peace shall embrace you as friend,
long lost; now found.

(Micah 4:6–8)

Silence

With the need for love within our heart, we come to
this day ever mindful of the friends who have been a
gift in our life. We pray for all those who are lonely or
who despair of true friendship. With their needs
foremost in our heart, we offer our intentions to the
God who bears us nothing but good . . .

The Lord's Prayer

Canticle

Offering

Closing

EVENING PRAYER

Presence

Each night, darkness comes upon us. But our fear of loneliness can be calmed, for in our midst is the Holy One whose tender love has brought us salvation and peace. This night we pray for an increase of the gift of loving friends in our life. We give God thanks for the goodness of those who call us friends as well.

Prayer

O God, your life
is itself the friendship of all creation.
From the beginning, you made the world
in the image of your life of love.
Evening has fallen across the earth,
and we are reminded
of how you have embraced us
        with a blanket of tender care.
The darkness, however, further reminds us
of those who live in shadows,
surrounded by fear and doubt,
almost paralyzed to give or accept
the gift of your love offered from human friends.
In our streets and sometimes in our homes,
there are those who live among us
and feel unloved and unwanted.
Send your light into our life.
Move us to seek out the lost and the lonely,
the despairing and those hungry for compassion.
Help us to embrace them and make them our friends.
Increase your gift of friendship in our life
and make us bold to befriend the whole world.
We ask this through Christ and the Holy Spirit,
with you, One God, forever and ever.
Amen.

Before every other truth in the world,
know this word from my heart:
There is no greater love in all creation
than to lay down your life for your friends.
I have gathered you from streets and cities
to call you my dearest friends.
You are indeed my friends
if you obey my one commandment:
love one another
as I have loved you.
In days gone by,
I sometimes called you servants.
I sometimes made you pupils.
But slaves and students
do not know their teachers well.
This night I call you friends
for you know now all that I have known from God.
You did not choose me.
I chose you.
I chose you to bear fruit for a hungry world.
Go forth from me and bear fruit.
And live my one commandment:
Love one another as I have loved you.

(John 15:13–17)

Silence

God, you are the refuge and healing for every broken
heart. This night we remember the gift of friendship in
our life. We remember those who are lonely or bitter.
We bring their needs before you as we ask you to be
mindful of these special intentions . . .

The Lord's Prayer

Canticle

Offering

Closing

Second Thursday:
For Our Enemies
and Those We Have Harmed

**MORNING
PRAYER**

Presence

As another day calls us to life and labor, we bring into the presence of God the memories of broken friendships, of enemies who have hurt us, and the painful reminder that we too have hurt and angered others. In the spirit of Jesus who forgave and healed, we pray this day for all those with whom we are not yet at peace.

Prayer

O God, you created us in love
and desire all people to live in peace and harmony.
Despite the words of your prophets
and your invitations to justice,
we confess to the presence of enemies in our life.
We know that war does not begin with weapons.
Rather, our aggressions begin with human hate.
Through the course of our life,
we have known the jealousies and pettiness
that have led us away from your command to love.
Harsh can be our bitter thoughts.
Fearfully we remember how we have angered others.
May our prayer for conversion
lead us to peaceful reconciliation.
This day we beg you to make us more mindful
of the spirit of Christ who calls us to forgive
        and be forgiven.
Do not allow us to remain stubbornly resentful,
but give us the strength to offer your embrace of peace
to those we still call enemy.
We ask this through Christ and the Holy Spirit,
with you, One God, forever and ever.
Amen.

I hear your cries coming loudly from your mouths.
Why do you cry out in pain?
Why are you exhausted with bitter memories?
Do you not have a leader in your midst
who has shown you the way of forgiveness,
the path of peace?
Where are your hearts
that you have forgotten the counsel of your God
who calls you to forgive others
in the measure in which you have been forgiven?
If you will not heed my words
and follow in my justice,
then indeed you shall remain in your pain
and suffer the slavery of bitter memories.
O daughter of Zion, you writhe in childbirth.
Do not bring the child of wicked bitterness
        into this world.
Bring to birth the child of forgiveness and compassion.
Be steeped in the memory of your own transgressions.
Remember your own need of rescue.
And then, remembering your need,
I will bring you out with tender love
to offer your loving to those who have harmed you.

(Micah 4:9–10)

Silence

Day has brought into light the harsh reality of the ways
we have harmed others and the ways we have been
harmed. In Jesus, we are called to conversion of life, to
extend the gift of God's reconciliation to every human
being. We bear up these needs to God as we offer our
special intentions . . .

The Lord's Prayer

Canticle

Offering

Closing

**EVENING
PRAYER**

Presence

Nighttime is with us once again. In the shadow of the
evening, we are reminded of the darker side of the
human heart. We remember the bleak times when we
have sown the seeds of human hatred and jealousy.
This night we bring to God those who have hurt us
and those we ourselves have caused to suffer. We pray
for an end to our separation from them, and for a
beginning of reconciliation.

Prayer

O God, when Jesus came into our world,
there was no time at which Christ did not embrace
the full range of our human living.
Born into a human family, Jesus knew the risks
    of our life.
Surrounded by loving friends,
Jesus also had enemies.
This night we call to mind the memory
    of that final supper.
At that meal, there was one
who dipped the hand of betrayal
into the dish of friendship.
Jesus knew the pain of broken trust
and suffered at the hands of those
who earlier in the week
had raised their voices with joyful hosannas.
Yet from the cross of Christ,
    there was no condemnation,
only the gift of forgiveness and peace.
Bathe us now with those same gifts
    from the side of Christ.
With your grace may we be forgiving
and able to ask forgiveness from those we have harmed.
Teach us again to live in peace with one another.
We ask this through Christ and the Holy Spirit,
with you, One God, forever and ever.
Amen.

I have given you my commandment:
Love one another.
Yet to live in my love
will not protect you from the world's hatred.
As the world has hated me and my truth,
so you can expect the same.
But be consoled.
For the world has hated me long before it hated you.
But why? Why should this world hate you?
Why does the world raise its hand against you?
The reason is this:
You do not belong to the spirit of this world.
You were not brought to birth in the power
    of the world.
I chose you from out of this world as my witnesses.
Remember then what I have told you:
no servant can be greater than the master.
If the world has driven me,
then the world will drive and harry you.
They will respect your words
in the measure they have respected mine.
Be strengthened then in my commandment:
Love one another as I have loved you.

(John 15:18–20)

Silence

God of love and peace, this night we call to mind those
who have been our enemies, those who have caused us
suffering and pain. We remember well that we too have
been instruments of sorrow for others. And so we ask
that you call us and our enemies to conversion and to
a new peace between us. With this, we bear now our
special needs before you . . .

The Lord's Prayer

Canticle

Offering

Closing

Second Friday:
For Repentance
of the Discord We Create

Presence

A new day has come upon us, and new opportunities to live the Gospel are offered to us. This day we call to mind the moments of our life where we have failed to see the presence of Christ. We bring to prayer the discord we create in our communities when we fail to bear witness to the justice and peace of Christ Jesus.

Prayer

O God, each day you bring us new possibilities
for the proclamation of your peace and justice.
Not limited to our human imagination,
in every age you go beyond our thoughts
and invite us to deeper insight into the wisdom
     of your loving.
This day we confess our failure
to gather our life together in peace,
to carve laws more in keeping with your mercy,
to build up our society in justice and harmony.
Too often fear, greed, and pride have led us to forget
the presence of the poor and the widowed,
the orphan and the stranger.
Countless homeless people wander our streets
while we pursue our own security.
Stir up your Spirit in our midst.
Speak your voice of caring
to governments and every human gathering
so that our life in this world
will reflect the gospel commitment
to tend the wounded and set the captives free.
We ask this through Christ and the Holy Spirit,
with you, One God, forever and ever.
Amen.

And you, Bethlehem-Ephrathah,
you are the smallest of the cities of Judah.
Though you are counted as lowly,
it will be from your womb
that an Anointed shall be born.
This One shall rule my people Israel,
and they shall wonder as to my Anointed's origins.
This is the ancient, promised leader
whose presence shall be a contradiction
to the powers and princes of the world.
My Anointed shall love as I love.
My Anointed shall rule as a gentle shepherdess
whose loving, ever faithful and vigilant care
shall seek out and save the wandering lamb.
But like the watchful shepherd,
my Anointed shall stand firm
and defend the poor and the lowly.
No need shall escape that Watcher's eye,
that heart ready to defend.
The greatness of my Anointed
shall extend over the whole earth.
And all the people shall be secure.
For them, my Anointed shall be peace!

(Micah 5:1–3)

Canticle

Silence

Conscious that each day Yahweh leads us to new
challenges to be met with Gospel-love, we remember
our societies and nations. Though we are too often
slow to love and defend the poor, the voice of Christ
bids us beyond our failures into a new day of justice.
In this spirit of repentance for the seeds of discord
that we spread, we offer our special needs to the
mercy of God . . .

Offering

The Lord's Prayer

Closing

EVENING PRAYER

Presence

Another day has ended. We have brought to a close the work of our hands. This night we reflect upon the paths that we and our societies have walked this day. Asking for the courage of the Holy Spirit, we lay our conscience open before God's judgment so that we may see the charity we have avoided and stand ready to be brought to a deeper commitment.

Prayer

O God, you have loved us as your special people,
graced with gifts and blessings.
Yet our flesh is weak, our minds limited.
Even when our spirits would make us bold,
our hands fail to serve your truth and mercy.
This night we remember the many ways
that your Gospel-love is yet unlived.
We recall how often our own actions
stand in the way of justice and peace.
To love as you love us in Christ
is not a simple task.
The burdens of this world
can often stand as obstacles to our courage
and temptations to our wayward spirits.
Breathe the spirit of repentance into our hearts.
Make us bold to call our world
to the task of feeding the hungry, of clothing the naked,
of proclaiming the good news of Christ's liberty
    to the lowly.
Do not permit us to let any power stifle our hearts.
We ask this through Christ and the Holy Spirit,
with you, One God, forever and ever.
Amen.

Do not be afraid or surprised.
For what they have done to me
they will do to you as well.
All this they will do to you
because you love my name.
The spirit of this world knows nothing
of the power of my God.
And though I have been faithful
and spoken God's word all my days,
yet the world covers its ears
and rebels against hearing the word of life.
Not for weakness is the world at sin
but for refusing to listen to the word.
How easy it is to hear your voice alone.
How difficult it is to open both ears and heart
to listen to the voice of God
that comes from smallest places of one's life.
Thus, the spirit of the world has hated me.
And because you love me,
it will hate you also.
But remember I am with you
as the one who gives you a new commandment:
Love one another as I have loved you.

(John 15:21–24)

Silence

Though quick to serve our own needs, we are often too slow to reform our laws and customs to serve the needs of those who are most deprived in life. This night we confess a sluggish spirit that leads our communities to fail in Gospel-love. Knowing full well the mercy of God who will lead us beyond our failures, we offer our special needs in prayer . . .

The Lord's Prayer

Canticle

Offering

Closing

Second Saturday:
For Those Held
in Apathy and Fear

Presence

Another day has come to us as a gift. We remember the presence of apathy and fear that can hold us prisoner and keep us from living the full measure of God's peace and justice. We pray this day that the Holy Spirit will urge us to charity and calm our fears. We hope and pray that God will quicken our living out the message of Christ in our midst.

Prayer

O God, we are far from your perfect children.
At times it seems our very flesh weighs us down
from rising from our slumber
to the voices of the poor and the dispossessed.
Even Jesus knew fatigue and weariness of spirit.
Yet Christ did not shrink from fear
but embraced the full measure of human needs,
even to tasting terror at death's door.
Without the help of your Spirit,
we can do nothing.
Without your grace,
we are prisoners to fear and apathy.
Break through our lack of caring.
Dismiss the spirit of terror from our hearts.
With your grace, may our nightmares cease
to frighten us away from each day's invitations to love.
Make us a strong and faithful people
who are quick to deeds of mercy, peace, and justice.
We ask this through Christ and the Holy Spirit,
with you, One God, forever and ever.
Amen.

The remnant of Jacob and Rachel shall be
a faithful people in all the world.
My people shall stand firm before every nation.
Against the forces of fear I shall be with them.
Like heaven-sent rains providing refreshment
I will allow my justice to rain on the world
through the presence of my people Israel.
Surely fear has blinded my world.
And the cries of the unloved have often been unheard.
But I shall raise up a strong nation
to tend the weak and sorrowing,
to bind up the wounds of the afflicted.
With the strength of the lion
and the loud cry of the lion's mate,
my voice shall be heard from the midst of my people,
a voice that announces peace and mercy
where before there had only been slavery and fear.
I shall raise up the glory of my people
and the oppressors of the world shall be no more.

(Micah 5:6–8)

Silence

This new day has brought us more invitations of grace.
As we begin this day, we pray that our apathy and fears
do not keep us from the work of mercy and justice. In
this spirit, we offer our special needs to the God who
strengthens the works of our hands . . .

The Lord's Prayer

Canticle

Offering

Closing

**EVENING
PRAYER**

Presence

We have come to the conclusion of another day with
the grace of Christ that brings our deeds of mercy to
fullness. Tonight we repent the many ways that we
have chosen not to care for the needy. We confess our
fears and apathy, and we ask for God's strength to go
beyond them.

Prayer

O God, you did not create us to be alone and fearful.
You created us to extend your loving care
to every creature of our world.
So many times your prophets
called an uncaring world to repentance,
fearful hearts to the tasks of loving.
Because you love us so much,
you did not shrink from our world
nor stay distant from our needs.
Boldly you moved into our midst
as the Word made flesh, resplendent in mercy.
This night and forever,
move in our heart.
Drive out our fear
and every form of selfishness
that keeps us from caring for the poor and lowly
as your special people, the new remnant of Israel.
We ask this through Christ and the Holy Spirit,
with you, One God, forever and ever.
Amen.

In the beginning was the Word
and the Word was with God
and the Word was God.
The Word leapt from the mouth of God
and brought to life
every star and planet,
every rock and tree,
every animal and bird,
every woman and man,
every living thought and movement.
The Word leapt from the mouth of God
and did not amble away from the fullness of our life.
No, this Word became our flesh.
And the glory of the Word lives among us,
enlightening our days
and illumining our nights.
"And now," says the Word, "Another is coming."
"One who is your advocate and strength,
who will lead you into the fullness of mercy and peace,
that you yourselves might leap into the world
and bring its flesh again to my justice."
And the new commandment to us is this:
Love one another as Christ has loved us.

(John 1:1–18; 15:26–27)

Silence

Everlasting God, this night we bring before you a
weak and sinful heart. Weighed down by apathy and
fear, we have too easily walked away from those in need
of generous mercy. Repentant, we ask your spirit of
conversion to come upon us as we bring our needs
to your love . . .

The Lord's Prayer

Canticle

Offering

Closing

Third Week
To Walk Humbly

Third Sunday:
For the Gifts of
Self-knowledge and Acceptance

Presence

A new day and a new week have come upon us with the gifts of light and peace. God invites us today to celebrate the gifts that are planted within us. As we wake from sleep, we pray for an increase in self-knowledge and self-acceptance. May our prayers this day strengthen us to be fully alive and, therefore, fully the glory of God.

Prayer

O God, our creator,
you formed us as women and men,
equal partners in the stewardship of your world:
joined forever as sisters and brothers,
yet within each of us lives a rich diversity
of different gifts, different hopes,
and different limitations.
In Jesus, your word born fully in our flesh,
you have seen and loved in us
all that you have made us to be.
Though graced, we are limited and often weak.
But our weaknesses themselves
are no obstacle to your passion for us.
Teach us to see in ourselves
what you have seen in each of us from birth.
Teach us to know our gifts and limits.
Keep us confidently on the path of self-knowledge,
fullness of wisdom, and joy in being your children.
We ask this through Christ and the Holy Spirit,
with you, One God, forever and ever.
Amen.

Comfort, give words and deeds of comfort
to my people who have suffered with despair!
Jerusalem, my beloved people,
my tender love is poured out upon you.
Your fear has come to an end.
No more shall you know guilt for your life.
Your doubts are expiated and blotted out.
Indeed, I lavish you doubly as my precious ones.
A voice cries out in the desert:
"Prepare the way of the Most High.
Make a clean, straight path in the wasteland
for the knowledge of God is coming close.
Every pride shall be lowered;
every doubt filled in,
for the glory of God shall be revealed
in the flesh of a people who dance for joy."

(Isaiah 40:1–5)

Silence

Blessed God, you have made us in your image and filled us with every grace and blessing. We pray today for an increase in self-knowledge that we may do your will with clearer vision. As people desiring more and more to be your faithful servants, we offer to you these special needs . . .

The Lord's Prayer

Canticle

Offering

Closing

**EVENING
PRAYER**

Presence

As evening draws close, we are brought into the light of Jesus Christ. May we be strengthened by the memory of Jesus' Resurrection and his reassurances to the scared and desperate disciples. We pray for a greater acceptance of our gifts, our limits, and our call to be instruments of peace and servants of Christ Jesus.

Prayer

O God, this is the time of our salvation.
Jesus still breathes the legacy of peace upon us
just as he did those first friends and witnesses
who doubted and despaired
that your word to them was true,
that their lives could know your grace.
This night we look clearly into the mirror of our life
and find there gifts and limits,
grace and sin, firm knowledge and human doubts.
We shrink from loving ourselves
and from embracing the fabric of our life.
But Christ did not hesitate to embrace us
with healing touch, on the wood of the cross,
in his rising, and along the road to Emmaus.
By that embrace, Jesus sealed forever
your ancient promises of eternal peace and salvation.
Raise us from our fears.
Deflate our false pride.
Teach us to accept ourselves.
Help us to let your Holy Spirit use our gifts and limits
for the glory of your name.
We ask this through Christ and the Holy Spirit,
with you, One God, forever and ever.
Amen.

Blessed are you, the poor,
the peace of God is yours.
Blessed are you, the sorrowing,
the healing of heaven is poured upon you.
Blessed are you, the lowly,
indeed you shall be raised up.
Blessed are you, the hungry and thirsty,
the food of life shall feed you.
Blessed are you, the merciful,
mercy shall be yours.
Blessed are you, the devoted,
the vision of God's love is yours.
Blessed are you, the peaceful,
the gift of peace is yours.
Blessed are you, the persecuted,
the justice of God is your heritage.
Blessed are you when you suffer for my sake,
the justice of God shines through you.
Be glad and rejoice!
The strong presence of God is your blessing!

(Matthew 5:3–12)

Silence

O God, our hearts will never rest until they come to
your peace. Tonight we pray that we may love ourselves
as you have made and loved us; that we may embrace
our different gospel paths to which you have called us.
Asking for the gift of self-acceptance, we also bring to
you our special intentions . . .

The Lord's Prayer

Canticle

Offering

Closing

Third Monday:
For the Gifts of Wisdom
and Discernment

**MORNING
PRAYER**

Presence

At the beginning of this day, we are sharply aware that
our human knowledge is limited and that all wisdom
comes from the Holy Spirit. Our life draws dignity and
grace from the love of Jesus present among us. And so
we come before God, asking for an increase of divine
wisdom in our life so that our every work may announce that justice and peace come from God alone.

Prayer

O God, at the dawn of creation
you breathed your spirit into the dust of earth
and brought into being the glory of our life.
We have grown to this day,
using your many gifts
in the cause of human progress and knowledge.
Yet we have failed.
Too often our learning has brought suffering.
Our progress has often been a sad hindrance
      to your justice,
with no peace for the poor and the lonely.
As daylight breaks,
we beg for the power of your Spirit
to breathe upon us once again.
Add your holy wisdom to our learning.
Temper our technology with your mercy
and never let us use the gift of learning
to take away the gift of life that is yours alone to give.
Give us wisdom in our time, Holy One!
We ask this through Christ and the Holy Spirit,
with you, One God, forever and ever.
Amen.

82

Canticle

A voice thunders: "Cry out full throated."
And I answer in return: "What shall I cry?"
The voice thunders: "Remember you are grass.
Neither more nor less, like grass of the field.
Left alone to your own devices,
your glory, like a summer flower,
is here today and gone the next.
It passes, withers, and dies.
Only with the breath of God does the flower live.
Only with the gift of wisdom does the world turn.
Too often you forget
and build yourselves an empire
that, in the end, must crumble.
For life itself is the gift of God alone,
every living thing draws life from God's mouth.
If God takes back that breath you die.
Like the grass of the summer field,
like the flower of the autumn garden,
so it is with you,
that without the life of God within you,
you wither and die and are no more."
But the wisdom of God is life itself.
The word that lives forever!

(Isaiah 40:6–8)

Silence

Offering

As we return this day to our labor and learning, we
remember that it is the gift of wisdom alone that gives
dignity and life to the work of our hands and the
pursuit of human knowledge. We pray this day that
God's holy wisdom will grace our every effort and
inspire us to let justice and peace be the foundation of
human progress. In this spirit, we bring our needs before
the God of all . . .

Closing

The Lord's Prayer

EVENING PRAYER

Presence

Once again darkness has fallen, and another day is drawing to a close. As the shadows lengthen, we are called to reflect upon the new places the Spirit may be leading us. We pray too that we may be given the gift of discernment to know the new paths down which God may be calling us.

Prayer

O God, you design the whole universe
and from your life-giving hands
you form the structure of our life.
You did not create us to be a waste
or our lifetime to be formless.
You have created our hands and heart
to be the hands and heart of Christ in our world.
As this day draws to a close,
we remember the many nighttimes of our life
when the spirit of confusion kept us from detecting
the path you were calling us to walk.
In the waters of baptism, you consecrated us all.
You made us a race of priests, prophets, and stewards
to go forth in equality of grace
to preach the Good News in diverse and blessed ways.
This night, inspire us to see your will in our life.
Grant us the gift of discernment.
Never let us ignore your invitations to grace.
Help us to see your beloved Jesus
calling us to new pathways of life and service.
We ask this through Christ and the Holy Spirit,
with you, One God, forever and ever.
Amen.

You are the salt of the earth.
But what if salt goes flat?
How can you restore and bring back the taste?
Flat salt can only be discarded and ground underfoot.
It has no use.
You are the light of the world.
You are a city set upon a hill.
Cities on the heights cannot be hidden.
Wise people do not hide their lamps.
They do not put candles under bushel baskets.
They take their lamps and raise them up.
They place their lamps on lamp stands
where they give light to the whole house.
In this same way, your life must be a light.
Your goodness must shine before the world
as gifts to people who walk in darkness
so that they may give the gift of praise
to the God who is the source of every goodness.

(Matthew 5:13–16)

Silence

Loving and gracious God, daily we struggle to know
your will, to discern the varied paths to which you call
us for the service of the world and the good of your
people. As this day comes to an end, we ask for inspiration. We ask that we may hear your voice. In this spirit
of openness, we bring our many needs before you . . .

The Lord's Prayer

Canticle

Offering

Closing

Third Tuesday:
For the Gifts
of Patience and Courage

Presence

Daylight has come upon us, and we are called again to our daily work. We know full well how easily we can become disheartened by setbacks. At the start of this new day, we pray for the gifts of patience and courage to hold fast to your word through times of suffering and conflict.

Prayer

God of every goodness,
we are grateful for your loving presence in our life.
You are our constant and faithful companion
and remain close to us even when we are unfaithful.
Truly you are the God of patience,
the God who suffers with our every weakness.
You are not distant from your creation,
from the work of your hands.
You live and move and have your being
within the progression of our history.
In the fullness of all time,
you sent your beloved Jesus as a seal of your loving.
Jesus suffered with us.
Jesus journeyed with us
and embraced, in all love, the terror of our dying.
With the presence of Christ among us,
teach us the gift of patience and strengthen us.
Help us to be truly present to one another
        in joy and grief
as you are present to us all the days of our life.
We ask this through Christ and the Holy Spirit,
with you, One God, forever and ever.
Amen.

Go up onto the mountains.
Go up to the top of Mount Zion.
Be the herald of a new justice, a new virtue.
Go up and shout at the top of your voice.
Shout to the people that fear has come to an end.
Tell them that their loneliness and exile are over.
Announce to the people of Judah
that their God is in their midst:
the God who has suffered with them,
the God who has heard their cries,
the God who has tasted the salt of their tears.
Here is their God among them.
Here is the God of might and gentleness,
the God who rules with a strong but tender arm.
The rewards of God are many.
The graces and blessings of the Most High are rich.
Like a shepherdess, God tends the lambs.
Like a shepherd, God leads the flock,
carrying the newborn lambs,
leading the ewes and rams.

(Isaiah 40:9–11)

Silence

Canticle

On this day of grace, we recall that the patience of God
is a gift. It is not lived easily. Yet we know that our God
is a patient and loving God, a God who has suffered
with us and asks us to share compassion with our sisters
and brothers. In the spirit of true patience, we offer our
needs this day . . .

Offering

The Lord's Prayer

Closing

EVENING PRAYER

Presence

At the end of this day, we marvel at what the grace of God has brought about in our life. We realize that the path of Christian life demands courage. It is not easy to live a just and peaceful life. The fortitude of the spiritual life is itself a gift from a God whose strength topples the powers of pride and raises up the lowly. This night we pray for an increase of godly strength in our life, and in the life of all those who would be witnesses of Jesus Christ.

Prayer

God of heaven and earth,
your strength is coupled with compassion,
your strong arm is clothed in tender love and justice.
When your people cried out to you from slavery,
you did not let their cries go unheard.
You led them forth
and brought them to your promise as a new nation,
a people called to mercy and tender love.
Tonight we remember the poor and the dispossessed.
We remember how often our love and care of them
        is weak.
We confess that we shrink from their service
and from nurturing peace upon the earth.
Breathe forth your spirit of fortitude and strength.
In Christ, make us bold witnesses
to stand before the powers of this world,
the forces that devise new forms of slavery.
Give us the strength to be faithful
as Jesus is the faithful witness in our midst.
We ask this through Christ and the Holy Spirit,
with you, One God, forever and ever.
Amen.

Do not think I have come into your midst
to do away with the message of the prophets
or the deep spirit of the law.
I am in your midst as the holy one
who brings your laws to fulfillment.
On my holy mountain I gave you my word, my law;
carved on stone, it was handed to Moses.
From the lips of the prophets you heard words of mercy.
Solemnly I tell you,
until heaven and earth pass away,
not the smallest letter of the law will be lost.
Be strong then and heed my words.
For if you count yourself as holy,
if you would fulfill my law
then your love must grow ever stronger.
If your holiness of life will go no deeper
than the lying words of hypocrites,
then you shall not enter the fullness of God's Reign.

(Matthew 5:17–20)

Silence

Gently present God, we realize that the pathway of
your truth is difficult. Indeed, without the strength of
Jesus in our midst, it would be impossible to stay faithful
to your justice and peace. This night we remember the
need for your courage in our life. Acknowledging our
need, we mention now these special intentions . . .

The Lord's Prayer

Canticle

Offering

Closing

Third Wednesday:
For the Gifts of Charity
and Compassion

Presence

Daylight has come. This new day is calling us from our sleep to the daily work of God's justice and peace. We pray in this morning hour for an increase of charity and love in our life. We pray that we may be open to loving others with that same affection that Jesus offered to the disciples, and even to his enemies.

Prayer

O God, it was no cold or dry spirit
that led you to create our universe
or form men and women in your image.
No, it was with the passion of tender love
that you spoke, and your word made all that is!
As you formed the chosen people,
you stayed intimately by their side
and never failed to speak to them
of an anointed leader
who would be the fulfillment of your promises
of justice, love, and peace.
Today we hear the call of Jesus in our midst.
We hear Jesus prompting us to love others
as we have been loved by the Suffering Servant.
We acknowledge and confess our selfishness,
and we fear love's demands.
Through the power of your Holy Spirit,
kindle a fire in our hearts and make us loving people
whose passion for each other
    reflects the passion of Christ.
We ask this through Christ and the Holy Spirit,
with you, One God, forever and ever.
Amen.

Here is my servant whom I raise up.
The Chosen One in whom I am delighted,
in whose heart I have placed my spirit.
The One who shall bring forth justice in the land
as a flower comes up surprisingly in the desert.
My servant shall not cry out in pride,
shall not raise a strident voice in the streets.
My servant shall not shout the message of my heart
but shall speak my word in gentleness of spirit.
My Chosen One shall be so gentle
as not to break the smallest reed,
nor bruise the newest tendril of a vine,
nor quench the smoldering wick on a candle!
But with a strong arm and a mighty heart of love,
my Chosen One shall go forth
to establish justice, love, and peace
        upon the whole earth.
The coastlands and the steppe,
the nations and the cities
shall wait upon my Chosen's word of life!

(Isaiah 42:1–4)

Canticle

Silence

As women and men who have been brought to a new
birth of loving by water and the Spirit, we come before
God this day, asking for the blessing of abiding charity
in our life. Knowing how frail this gift can be, we ask
that we be strengthened with the spirit of Christ whose
love was never weak. In this spirit, we present our
special needs and intentions . . .

Offering

The Lord's Prayer

Closing

EVENING PRAYER

Presence

Another day has come to an end. The challenges and blessings of our workday have been left behind. We gather in the spirit of petition to ask God to increase our compassion for others. We have been touched by the sights, sounds, and smells of those who live home-less and orphaned, without human companionship and care. We pray that Christ will make us courageous so we can help them in their need for human warmth and love.

Prayer

O God, you are the origin of love
and the source of human affection.
Living in your love
does not protect us from the troubles of this life.
Following in your pathways of peace
is no guarantee that we will never suffer.
You sent Jesus among us;
and in his compassion,
you bound yourself as closely as possible
to the cries of the poor and the hopelessness
    of the hungry.
When Jesus stretched out his arms upon the cross,
all of humanity was gathered up
into the passion you have for our good.
This night and forever, increase in our life
the blessing of compassion.
You gather us when we are most lonely and afraid.
Do not let us fear to do the same for others.
Help us to share the gift of compassion.
In our loving, may your love be seen.
Open our heart and hands to those in need.
We ask this through Christ and the Holy Spirit,
with you, One God, forever and ever.
Amen.

You have heard the old commandment:
"You shall not commit murder;
every murderer shall be brought to judgment."
Now I give you a new commandment.
What I say to you is this:
If you grow angry with your sister,
you shall be brought to judgment.
If you abuse your brother in speech or word,
you shall be brought before the people.
If you hold anyone in contempt,
you shall risk the fires of Gehenna.
If you come to offer your sacrifice,
and suddenly remember
that someone has a grievance against you,
leave your gift at the altar and be reconciled.
After making peace, then come back
and give your gift to God.
Your love and your holiness of life
must go deeper than the lying words of hypocrites.
(Matthew 5:21–25)

Silence

God of love, the poor and the lonely wander our
streets, afraid and angry at their tremendous want. This
night we pray: never permit us to forget their need;
never let us turn our back on people in need of human
compassion and care. As we pray for the gift of compassion in our life, we offer these special needs . . .

The Lord's Prayer

Canticle

Offering

Closing

Third Thursday:
For the Gifts
of Inspiration and Strength

Presence

Another day has dawned, and with it comes unexpected invitations for grace and blessings. We pray that Christ in our midst will keep our heart and mind open to new understandings and fresh ways of living out the gospel message of justice and peace. With the courage of the Holy Spirit alive in us, we will resist the temptations to hardness of heart.

Prayer

O God, on every page of the sacred Scriptures
we find your divine heart overflowing
with unexpected graces and blessings for the world.
You are God, unlimited by our human logic,
unchained by human ways.
You created us in your image.
You fashioned a chosen people
from a band of escaped, wandering slaves.
You brought to birth a savior
from a nation impoverished and small.
In every age, your gift of inspiration
leads artists and scientists and builders
to dream new dreams and imagine fresh visions.
This day, breathe your inspiration into us.
Invade our inert heart with your gentle movements.
In the spirit of Christ among us,
help us to give up our clinging to the past
and become a witness to your voice that proclaims:
"Behold! I make all things new."
We ask this through Christ and the Holy Spirit,
with you, One God, forever and ever.
Amen.

But now, thus says our God,
the God who created you and redeemed you,
the God who formed you from nothing:
"Fear not, for I have redeemed you.
I have called you by your name and you are mine.
If you pass through driving waters, I will be with you.
If you are swept up in roiling rivers, you will not drown.
If you were to walk through raging fires,
you would not be burned.
I am your God, the mighty one,
the holy one of Israel,
the one who brings you to salvation.
I would give away nations for you.
I would offer peoples and the wealth of creation
as a ransom for your life.
Because you are precious in my eyes.
You are my beloved, my glorious love.
For you I would give the whole world
and offer many in exchange for your life."

(Isaiah 43:1–4)

Silence

As a new day comes, we are filled with the breath of
God that is our life and inspiration. Acknowledging
that we are nothing without the presence of Christ
among us, we pray this day for an increase of God's
inspiring love in our life. We pray that we may be open
to the movements of the Holy Spirit, and we offer these
special needs to the care of God's grace . . .

The Lord's Prayer

Canticle

Offering

Closing

EVENING PRAYER

Presence

Nighttime is upon us, and we reflect upon what we have done in God's name today. We ask that you, God, would bless us now and always with the gift of true courage to live out the message of Jesus that is justice and peace for the world.

Prayer

O God, our every action draws life from your heart.
Your love for sinful humanity is not a weak affection.
You brought your people out from slavery
with a strong arm and a mighty word.
Jesus walked in the streets of our lives
with a courage and bravery that went beyond
        human fears.
In water and the gift of the Spirit,
Jesus has called us to be courageous witnesses
of gospel justice and peace.
Yet we know the realities of fear and worry.
To be an instrument of peace in a world
        of martyred servants,
to claim the Gospel as our life
when a shallow grave may swallow up our years,
what price could be more exacting?
Yet, despite our questions and timid heart,
your Spirit moves us with new courage.
This night, put our fears to flight.
Take away our weakness.
Plant in us that blessing of gospel-courage
that leads slaves to your freedom
and brings the promise of life where once
        there was only death.
We ask this through Christ and the Holy Spirit,
with you, One God, forever and ever.
Amen.

Be on guard against empty piety.
Do not cling to hollow practices.
Do not perform your good deeds for entertainment.
If you give alms, give them in secret.
Do not announce your charity and goodness.
Do not pray like empty hypocrites
nor think that God demands a multitude of words.
Do not forgive the failures only of your friends.
Do not fast so that others can see.
Do not lay up riches for yourself in this life,
believing that wealth can bring you salvation.
Look at the birds of the air
who do not spin, nor sow, nor reap.
Yet God feeds them all.
So why do you worry about your life?
Can all your worry extend your years?
God is not a distant God,
nor a God who is content with empty faith.
Our God gives us daily bread,
and sees goodness in the secrets of our heart.
Your holiness of life must go deeper,
than the lying words of hypocrites.

(Matthew 6)

Silence

God of courage and compassion, at the end of this day
we come before you to pray for renewed courage to do
your holy will. We pray that this nighttime will refresh
us to continue to spread the gospel message when we
wake. In this spirit, we bring before you these special
needs . . .

The Lord's Prayer

Canticle

Offering

Closing

Third Friday:
For Repentance
of Personal Failures

Presence

The sun has risen on a new beginning to our labors for the justice and peace of the Reign of God. But the glory of this day brings with it the reminder that we sometimes sin. Despite our many efforts, we miss the mark and unleash the unkind word and the hurtful act. This day we pray in repentance for our personal failures and sins.

Prayer

O God, we are your people.
Unlike you, we are flesh and blood,
and we know the weaknesses of our spirits.
Through the ages, men and women
have strayed from your path of righteousness
and wandered into sinful ways.
Time and again you send us your reforming spirit,
Yet it seems we never learn.
We endlessly weave the pattern of sin.
Again, we confess our selfishness,
our lack of love,
our pride, and lust, and anger.
Yet we are not without hope.
Jesus taught us once for all
that you do not desire the sinner to die
but to come to newness of life.
Breathe your Spirit upon us this day.
Bring us always into the sunlight
        of your redeeming grace.
We ask this through Christ and the Holy Spirit,
with you, One God, forever and ever.
Amen.

The servant of Yahweh grew up like a sapling
    in our midst,
like a shoot from a parched and lifeless earth.
There was in this servant nothing beautiful of earth,
nothing comely that would be called attractive.
This servant was spurned and avoided; indeed, shamed.
This is the man of suffering,
like a mother of sorrows,
accustomed to bearing infirmity,
one of those from whom the living hide their face.
Spurned, we did not hold the servant of Yahweh
in any measure of human esteem or honor.
Yet, God's servant bore our infirmities and sufferings,
stricken for our sake and smitten,
pierced for our offenses and crushed for our sins,
taken up with our chastisement,
in whose wounds we have been healed.
God laid upon the head of this servant
the guilt and suffering of the world.

(Isaiah 53:2–6)

Canticle

Silence

Christ is life, love, and forgiveness. God desires our
turning away from all that is destructive and hopeless.
Through Christ Jesus the compassionate, we ask to be
renewed in the grace of healing, and we lay before God
our special needs and intentions . . .

Offering

The Lord's Prayer

Closing

EVENING PRAYER

Presence

At the beginning of this night, we remember the end of Christ's agony. The body of God's holy one was brought into the silence of the tomb. We remember how often our life is entombed in our selfishness, our sinful ways. We wait, like the dead Jesus, to be raised up to the fullness of grace. We pray for the power of the Spirit to move us beyond the nighttime of our sins and bring us to a new day of God's freedom and joy.

Prayer

O God, on Good Friday
Jesus opened wide his arms upon the cross
and gathered the sinfulness of all people
into the wider grace of redemption.
The death of Christ sealed that whole blessed life,
lived as a word of love incarnate in our midst.
Jesus gave a new command of love,
to be extended even to enemies.
Jesus showed the world
that your presence among us was not confined
        to human logic.
Jesus manifested your presence in the poor
        and the lonely,
in the wounded and the grieving,
in those that the world does not count as attractive.
We have been slow to see your presence,
slow to love as Jesus taught us.
We have been chained to our twisted logic
and refused your justice, mercy, and acceptance
to those we label strange or unacceptable.
Receive our sorrow for our sinful ways,
and draw us to a new dawn of life-giving love.
We ask this through Christ and the Holy Spirit,
with you, One God, forever and ever.
Amen.

You have heard an ancient law,
a commandment given to your forebears:
"Love your kinfolk and those who share your country.
Hate your enemy and those who do you harm."
But I give to you a new commandment,
a new law for future generations:
Love your enemy.
Care for those who have done you harm.
Pray for those who persecute you.
This will prove to the world
that you are truly children of God.
For does not God bring the sun to shine equally
on the wicked and the good, the just and the unjust?
Does not God bring the rain and mighty waters
to cleanse the just and the unjust, the wicked
        and the good?
Is your love no deeper than that of the hypocrites,
or the tax collectors who love only their own?
If you greet and love only those who wish
        and do you well,
what merit could there be in that?
In a word, do not set any boundaries on your goodness,
just as God does not limit divine mercy.
Your holiness of life must go deeper
than the lying words of hypocrites.

(Matthew 5:43–48)

Silence

Living God, tonight we come in the name of Jesus. We bring to you our many sins and failures, our inability to give flesh to the word of the Gospel. We stand in need of your redemption that alone can lead us out of our sinful ways and into grace and goodness. In this spirit, we bring you our special needs and intentions . . .

The Lord's Prayer

Canticle

Offering

Closing

Third Saturday:
For the Spirit of Ongoing
Conversion of Life

MORNING PRAYER

Presence

Daylight calls us from our sleep into the brightness of a new day. In every word and deed, Jesus called the people of Israel to a fresh covenant and an ongoing conversion of life. The Reign of God is at hand! This day we bring before God our need for the same spirit of conversion. With the blessing of true humility and joy, we ask God to renew our life in the spirit of the Gospel for the service of the world and one another.

Prayer

O God, our hearts are rarely content.
Despite all that we have, our hungers grow and multiply.
Ravaged by a lack of Christlike self-love,
we grasp for things beyond our reach.
We struggle in need of your conversion.
Our restless hearts need to be restless for your grace.
We need to lay our cares and our obsessions
within the loving heart of Jesus our brother
whose yoke is light, whose burden is pure joy.
This day we bring before you our discontented hearts.
We confess our need for your presence.
We ask that you breathe forth the power of your Spirit
and bring our faith to new fullness.
Keep us strong on our earthly pilgrimage.
Never let us believe that our human achievements
can ever exhaust the depths of your perfection.
May your Holy Spirit keep our hearts open
to the invitations of your grace.
We ask this through Christ and the Holy Spirit
with you, One God, forever and ever.
Amen.

The servant of Yahweh was treated harshly,
submitting to persecution without a word of complaint.
This servant was led like a lamb to the slaughter,
like a sheep dumb before the shearers,
silent, speaking no word or groan.
This servant was taken away,
oppressed and condemned,
not given another human thought,
cut off from the land of the living,
and struck down for the sins of the people.
Dead, the servant was assigned a common grave,
a burial among the wicked of the land.
This servant had done no wrong,
committed no sin, uttered no lies.
But this precious life was given as a ransom
    for the many,
an offering for sin.
Thus the servant of Yahweh will be raised up
with many descendants for future generations.
The will of God is revealed in this death,
and because of it our sins are forgiven.

(Isaiah 53:7–10)

Silence

At this morning hour, we delight in our call to be
disciples of Jesus, heralds of God's justice and peace.
May we open our heart in the spirit of ongoing conversion of life. This day, we pray for an increase of the
grace of redemption within us. And we bring to God
our special needs and intentions . . .

The Lord's Prayer

Canticle

Offering

Closing

**EVENING
PRAYER**

Presence

We have come to the end of another day and another week. We are grateful for the many blessings we have been given. Even so, we are painfully aware that our human limitations demand that we ask for the spirit of true conversion, the presence of Christ who can shepherd us beyond ourselves and lead us into newness of life and purpose. We ask God to refresh us and mold us anew in the love we have been asked to share with all the world.

Prayer

O God, you have brought us to the beginning
        of the night
and the end of another day of labor in your vineyard.
Your gift of sleep refreshes us
for the work of the Gospel.
Tonight we remember the restlessness of our heart,
the innate openness of spirit that marks
        our human endeavors.
Yet we cling to destructive ways.
We fail to acknowledge the prophetic words
that you send in the needs of your people.
Look upon us with love this night.
Hear our prayers for the spirit of conversion.
Do not allow us to dwell in self-satisfaction.
Rouse our human appetite
to hunger for the new life you are constantly creating
        in us.
Breathe forth the spirit of the Risen Jesus upon us.
Create us anew.
Help us to give witness to your will
that we may help others take the steps
        on their own journey
from a nighttime of doubt to the new day of your justice.
We ask this through Christ and the Holy Spirit,
with you, One God, forever and ever.
Amen.

You who hear my words and put them in practice
are like wise elders who build their homes on rock.
Rains fall, winds come, the torrents seize the beaches.
But though the forces shake the trees,
the houses of the wise remain untouched.
You who hear my words but do not put them
      into practice
are like the foolish of every age
who build their homes on sand.
Rains fall, winds come, the torrents seize the beaches.
And when the forces shake the trees,
the houses of the foolish fall!
They come to utter ruin.
You must build your life on rock
and live the word that I have preached.
For your holiness of life must go deeper
than the lying words of hypocrites.

                          (Matthew 7:24–27)

Silence

Canticle

God, you love the humble heart. Those who are
blessed with true humility know full well how much
they will always be in need of ongoing conversion of
life. So we pray for an increase in your transforming
grace. We pray to be a truly humble people, a people
who love themselves as God loves all of us, a people
who are willing to be transformed each moment by
your word. In this spirit, we give voice to our needs
and intentions . . .

Offering

The Lord's Prayer

Closing

Fourth Week
In Praise and Thanks

Fourth Sunday:
For the Gift of All Creation

Presence

This is the day of the new creation! Let us rejoice and
be glad. As the sun rises on this day of the Resurrection, we celebrate the gift of God's handiwork, the
creation of all that is. As we wake from our sleep, we
carry the gifts and mysteries of creation into the presence of God. For all that lives and all that breathes, we
give God praise.

Prayer

Loving Artist of creation,
we rise from sleep to give you praise.
From our hearts and homes
we look upon the array of creation,
and we delight in the beauty of our world,
the magnificence of the whole universe.
In the beginning, your love moved you
to speak the word and bring to birth
the sun and the moon, the stars and planets,
desert and steppe, ocean and river,
birds and beasts, women and men.
How many are the ways in which the richness
        of creation
reminds us of the deep and varied mysteries
        of your love for us!
As we recall the resurrection of Christ from the dead,
move us to sing your praises all the more.
Give us voices to proclaim your goodness
and to celebrate the gift of life
that you have given us to tend.
We ask this through Christ and the Holy Spirit,
with you, One God, forever and ever.
Amen.

Bless the God of heaven and earth,
All works of creation!
Praise and exalt God forever.
Angels and voices of the heavenly choirs,
give praise to the God of life.
Heavens above and vast stretches of creation,
give praise to the God of life.
All the waters above the heights of heaven,
give praise to the God of life.
All the hosts of the Mighty One of heaven,
give praise to the God of life.
Suns and moons, comets and constellations,
give praise to the God of life.
Stars and planets that spin and whirl,
give praise to the God of life.
Praiseworthy and glorious and exalted
is the God of all creation!

(Daniel 3:57ff.)

Silence

We are overjoyed at this celebration of the Resurrection of Jesus from the dead, and we give God praise for the works of creation. Our eyes see, our ears hear, our hands touch the presence of All Life, who moves in the beauty of our world and in the changing of every season. This day we gather our joy as one, and we present to God the many needs of creation as we offer these special intentions . . .

The Lord's Prayer

Canticle

Offering

Closing

EVENING PRAYER

Presence

This evening we remember with gratitude how Jesus came to those first friends in the upper room. Overcome with fear, how awestruck they must have been to see their teacher alive once again! We remember the many gifts of creation and give thanks for God's hands, which are always molding and guiding the life of the universe toward the day of justice and peace.

Prayer

Holy Creator,
you raised Jesus from the dead
and gave to your creation the fulfillment of all life.
Daylight is ending, but our heart is not afraid.
You, our God, make the light of Christ
burn brightly and everlastingly in our midst.
We are your people, your faithful remnant.
We gather from the corners of the world
      to wonder at your love.
You did not leave us orphans
nor allow us to suffer despair in the face
      of human death.
Instead you embraced the mystery of our pain
and sealed our lives with a new life
born beyond suffering's reach.
This night we give you thanks for Jesus
      alive in our midst.
We thank you for the many ways
that Jesus is present to us in every work of creation.
This night and forever, touch our heart
and grant us the spirit of true gratitude,
that our waking and sleeping
may find us breathing out thanksgiving
for all you have given us in creation.
We ask this through Christ and the Holy Spirit,
with you, One God, forever and ever.
Amen.

My soul and body magnify our God!
My spirit delights in the God who has saved us!
For God has looked upon this lowly servant
    with a just eye.
From this day and forever,
all the ages shall see me as truly blessed:
For the mighty and tender God of Israel
has done great things for me.
Holy is the name of Yahweh!
Mercy comes to those who are in awe of God.
Mercy flows from God to every age.
God has stretched out a mighty arm
scattering the proud who are chained by their conceit.
God has cast down the mighty of this world
raising up the lowly to new heights of glory.
God has sent the rich away with an empty belly,
filling the hungry and the poor with every good thing.
God has come to help our people Israel,
remembering the promise of mercy made long ago,
the ancient covenant made to our ancestors,
to Abraham, Sarah and their children forever!
                                        (Luke 1:46–55)

Silence

At this evening hour, Jesus breathed peace upon the
first disciples and promised them the Spirit, who would
make them bold witnesses of praise before the nations.
Gratitude fills us for the gifts of peace we have found in
creation. Thankful for our world's beauty, we offer our
needs and intentions to the God of everything that
lives and breathes . . .

The Lord's Prayer

Canticle

Offering

Closing

Fourth Monday:
For the Gift
of Redemption in Christ

Presence

As the sun rises, we are called to give God praise for the
gift of redemption that has come to us in the death and
the Resurrection of Jesus. God did not allow us to
journey through our days and nights alone and afraid.
Rather, taking on our flesh, God in Christ walks with
us and gives us the confidence to live in freedom and
justice. Remembering these many gifts, we are moved
this day to hearty praise.

Prayer

Loving and gracious God,
you are the source of all life and goodness.
You fashioned the glorious universe.
You created our human family
to raise our voices and speak the love that is your life.
In the fullness of time,
you sent Jesus into our midst,
born into a human family, born into our very flesh.
Though we had wandered far from your many graces,
you did not leave us,
but gave Jesus to us as your abiding presence
   in our world.
Loving God, this day we give you praise.
We praise you for the gift of redemption
that is ours in Christ.
Without this gift, we wither and die:
our voice becomes silent, our heart empty and dead.
Move us this day to speak your praise
before every living being.
Make our every action proclaim your goodness
until the day Christ comes again.
We ask this through Christ and the Holy Spirit,
with you, One God, forever and ever.

Amen.

Bless our God, all works of creation!
Every shower and dew that water the earth,
give praise to the God of life.
All winds and breezes that breathe across earth's face,
give praise to the God of life.
Fire that enlightens and heat that warms us,
give praise to the God of life.
Cold of winter and chill of the morning,
give praise to the God of life.
Morning dew and evening rains,
give praise to the God of life.
Frost of winter and winds that chill us,
give praise to the God of life.
Ice and snow and freezing storms,
give praise to the God of life.
Moon and night, sun and day,
give praise to the God of life.
Light of the daytime and darkness of night,
give praise to the God of life.
Streaks of lightning, thunder and clouds,
give praise to the God of life.
Praiseworthy and glorious and exalted
is the God of all creation!

(Daniel 3:57ff.)

Canticle

Silence

As we come to the beginning of yet another day, we are
aware that our life has new meaning and new hope
because we have been redeemed by Jesus. This day we
give God praise for the many graces of redemption that
we have come to know. In this spirit of joy, we offer to
God our special needs and intentions . . .

Offering

The Lord's Prayer

Closing

**EVENING
PRAYER**

Presence

Our day has come to a close. But our heart is never
closed to the grace we receive from the hands of Christ,
our redeemer. Without the gift of redemption in our
life, we would approach each night with terror and fear.
Burning brightly in our midst, the light of Christ is our
hope and our consolation. This night, we are filled
with thanksgiving for our redemption. We gather our
thoughts and prayers as one to give God thanks for
what has been accomplished in our midst through
Jesus' love for us.

Prayer

God of love, we give you deep thanks.
From the day of creation, you made us in freedom
and allowed us to wander in our own ways
even to abandon you and your good gifts.
We wandered, but you followed us
and untiringly matched our footsteps through history.
When your wisdom appointed it,
you sent Jesus, your word, into our world
to bring us back into your redeeming love
        and tender care.
In water and the Spirit, we have come to new life.
Our heart has been changed, our hopes refreshed.
If we give our life to the grace of your Spirit,
the shadows of human doubt and failure
cannot turn us aside from your promises.
This night we ask you to stir up the spirit of gratitude
        in our midst.
Our life is made joyful for the redemption of Christ,
which is our light and our peace.
Even in our sleeping,
may your spirit of thanksgiving grow within us.
And, when we wake from sleep, lead us back
        into our world
strengthened to witness to your word of salvation.
We ask this through Christ and the Holy Spirit,
with you, One God, forever and ever.
Amen.

I myself am the bread of life!
No one who comes to me shall ever be hungry,
no one who believes in me shall ever thirst.
But as I told you, though you see me,
you still do not believe in me.
All that our God has given me shall come to me.
No one who comes to me shall be rejected,
because it is not for me to reject the will
        of the one who sent me.
I have come from heaven
only to do the will of the one who sent me.
It is the will of God who sent me
that I should lose nothing of what I have been given.
Rather, that I should raise it up on the last day.
This is the will of my God,
the one who loves me more than father or mother:
that everyone who looks upon me and believes in me
shall come to eternal life
and shall be raised up on the last day.

(John 6:35–40)

Silence

Night has come again, but fear and doubt do not plague us. We remember with joy that in our midst is the holy one of Israel, Jesus, who has brought us the fullness of salvation. Bathed in the never-ending light of redemption, we bring our needs and intentions before the God who reads the movements of every hungry heart . . .

The Lord's Prayer

Canticle

Offering

Closing

Fourth Tuesday:
For the Gift of Loving

Presence

As this new day comes to its beginning, we remember
that a hunger for love has been placed deep within our
heart. We give God praise for this gift of loving that
leads us to extend our heart and hands to other men
and women. We give praise for the loving communion
of the human spirit that comes to us in family, friendship, and in the community of faith.

Prayer

God of all affection,
at the dawn of creation you placed
a hunger and a thirst for love within the human heart.
You did not desire us to be lonely
but gave us to one another as a gift and image
of the divine life you know within yourself.
Born into our flesh, reared in a human family,
taught to sing your praises in the communion of faith,
Jesus walked among us as a loved one
and taught us your ways of tenderness and passion.
With strong arms and a heart filled with care,
Jesus shared his life with us.
So great is your passion for us!
This day we give you praise for the love
that has come to us from you in our family,
        friends, and faith.
We ask that you stir up the power of your loving
so that we may burn with the same love for one another.
All praise be yours, God of loving passion.
We ask this through Christ and the Holy Spirit,
with you, One God, forever and ever.
Amen.

Let all the earth give praise to God,
give praise to the God of life.
Praiseworthy and glorious and exalted above all
is the God of all creation.
Mountains and hills and every high place of the earth,
give praise to the God of life.
Everything that grows from the soil and the land,
give praise to the God of life.
All springs and waters that give joy to eye and heart,
give praise to the God of life.
All seas and oceans and rivers,
give praise to the God of life.
All dolphins and fish who swim the mighty oceans,
give praise to the God of life.
All birds of the air and every winged creature,
give praise to the God of life.
All beasts of forest and farm,
give praise to the God of life.
All women and men and children of the earth,
give praise to the God of life.
Praiseworthy and glorious and exalted above all
is the God of all creation!

(Daniel 3:57 ff.)

Silence

As we embark upon a new day, we are filled with praise
for the loving unity of minds and hearts that we have
known from friends, family members, and those with
whom we share our life of faith. The mystery of human
love and passion is a gift from the God who is the
fountain of love. Conscious of the fragile nature of our
loving, we bring our needs and special intentions to
God this day . . .

The Lord's Prayer

Canticle

Offering

Closing

EVENING PRAYER

Presence

Night is once again with us. But our heart is filled with gratitude for the gift of human connection that has been given to us by God in Christ Jesus. Even when we doubt our ability to love or be loved in return, God has given us the presence of Jesus as our hope against the forces of loneliness and despair. Tonight we are filled with gratitude for the signs of love and affection that are a foretaste and promise of God's eternal love.

Prayer

O God, whose love feeds us forever,
we give you thanks this night
for the bright gift of Christ's light
that leads us from the nighttime of despair
to the dawn of your everlasting day of justice,
        love, and peace.
This night we are filled with gratitude
for the gifts of human love, passion, tenderness,
        and affection
that come to us so freely from your hands
and sustain us even when we doubt.
Our flesh longs for that tender touch
that crowns our work with appreciation,
that drives away the ache of loneliness,
and that makes us feel our worth as your children.
The presence of family, friends,
        and faith-filled companions
unites our hope with the hope of all the world.
Fill us with the spirit of gratitude for your love.
Move us to share your love with our sisters and brothers.
This night, receive our thanksgiving
and strengthen us to do your deeds of tender care
        in our world.
We ask this through Christ and the Holy Spirit,
with you, One God, forever and ever.
Amen.

I myself am the bread of life.
No one can come to me
unless God draws you into my life.
I will raise you up on the last day.
It is written in the prophets:
"They shall all be taught by God."
Everyone who has heard the call from God
comes to me in truth.
None of you has ever seen God directly.
Only the One who comes from God sees God fully!
Let me firmly assure you:
The one who has the gift of faith
is the one who has eternal life.
I myself am the bread of life!

(John 6:4–47)

Silence

Canticle

As we come to the beginning of another night, we are
filled with thanks for the many gifts we have been
given. We remember the love of friends, family, and
faith. Strengthened by our life's companions, we give
voice to our special needs and intentions . . .

Offering

The Lord's Prayer

Closing

Fourth Wednesday:
For the Gift of True Progress
Toward Justice and Peace

**MORNING
PRAYER**

Presence

As the sun rises and we are called again to life and
work, we offer God praise and adoration for the gift of
this new day. We are mindful of the many gifts that are
given to our human family. In a special way, we remember the progress made in the cause of justice and peace.
Today we offer our praise to God for the advances of
the human mind and spirit. We praise God for the
small, significant steps for peace that are made each day
by men and women of justice.

Prayer

Holy Wisdom, you are the fountain of human ingenuity.
You planted in our mind and heart
the thirst for truth
that has led us to probe the secrets of the universe
and the diverse riches of the human heart.
Praise to you, Holy Wisdom,
for the wonders of human progress
that are made each day.
Despite the setbacks we have seen in history,
the sad legacies of greed and lust,
our curiosity still leads us
down new avenues of learning.
Perfect each new invention,
each new discovery with your mercy.
Lead us to wonder at what can be born
when human endeavor and intelligence are twined
with your gifts of compassion and mercy.
We ask this through Christ and the Holy Spirit,
with you, One God, forever and ever.
Amen.

O house of Israel, faithful remnant,
give praise to the God of life.
People of faith,
give praise to the God of life.
Spirits and every soul of the just,
give praise to the God of life.
Holy women of every time and place,
give praise to the God of life.
Men of faith in every age,
give praise to the God of life.
Children whose voices sing with joy,
give praise to the God of life.
People of every nation and race,
give praise to the God of life.
Hananiah, Azariah, Mishael,
give praise to the God of life.
Exiles and those who thirst for justice,
give praise to the God of life.
Praiseworthy and glorious and exalted
is the God of all creation!

(Daniel 3:57 ff.)

Silence

At this new day, your people, O God, are filled with
wonder and praise for human progress, the steps we
take to make your vision of justice and peace come
true. The courageous people who resist the forces of
oppression and build up our world in your mercy fill us
with awe. In this spirit, we come before you and present
to you our needs and special intentions . . .

The Lord's Prayer

Canticle

Offering

Closing

EVENING PRAYER

Presence

As another night falls, we remember with gratitude the progress toward peace that has been made in our world this day. Admitting that we have not yet reached the fullness of God's peace and justice, we are grateful for even the small steps that have been taken. Filled with gratitude for the wonders of Christ's presence in our midst, we present ourselves to the God who is the origin of all human progress.

Prayer

O God, you are the inspiration of our every action
and the spring from which we draw wisdom
    and strength.
Without you we can do nothing.
Without your aid we can never build cities
    of justice and peace.
Our intentions are prone to shifting,
and sometimes we lack vision.
To point out to us the path of true righteousness,
you sent Jesus to show your mercy.
This night we give you heartfelt thanks
for even the small ways that your peace breaks out.
Though our laws and efforts do not yet match your will,
we are grateful for the Spirit of your wisdom
who has helped us to measure our life by your loving.
Fill us with gratitude
for the gifts of ingenuity and wisdom
that inspire people to make progress
    toward justice and peace.
Accept our thanksgiving and build us up
    each day and night
into the people that you call your own.
We ask this through Christ and the Holy Spirit,
with you, One God, forever and ever.
Amen.

I myself am the bread of life.
Your ancestors, wandering in the desert long ago,
ate manna that fell from the sky.
Even so, they died.
This is the true bread that comes down from heaven.
With the true bread that you will eat
you will never taste the power of death.
I myself am this living bread.
I have come down from heaven
as the new manna in your midst.
If you eat of this bread alone,
then indeed you shall live forever.
What is this bread that I give you?
The bread I give you for eternal life
is the gift of my very flesh.
I give my flesh for the life of the world.
I myself am the bread of life!

(John 6:48–51)

Silence

We have come to the end of another day. From the
many places where we work and live, we look out upon
our world, and we see the labor of the human mind and
human spirit exploring new means for the progress of
peace. Despite many obstacles, people throughout the
world have made efforts this day to bring justice and
equality to the suffering and the dispossessed. Grateful
for their efforts, we voice our needs and intentions to
God . . .

The Lord's Prayer

Canticle

Offering

Closing

Fourth Thursday:
For the Gift
of the Daily Gospel Challenge

Presence

The sun has risen, and we are called again from our
sleeping to a new day with new gifts and opportunities.
We are mindful that the life of faith is hardly without
challenges. The risks and invitations of grace are often
surprising and catch us unaware. Yet without their
uncomfortable presence, we would not grow and be
enriched. Today we give praise to God for the daily
challenges of Gospel-living.

Prayer

O God, you rightly deserve our words of praise.
From the day of our creation,
you made us to be like yourself.
Our living often becomes ordinary;
our daily life, seemingly commonplace.
Yet into our workaday world
you place new challenges and new opportunities
     of faith.
You sent our beloved redeemer
to surprise the nations out of their comfort
and the peoples from their ruts.
We give you praise for the challenges
     that have come our way,
the surprises and wonders that make our faith lively
and peak our imagination
to discover new paths of justice and peace.
Lift our voices to sing your praise.
Open our heart to accept the challenges
     of Gospel-living.
Do not let us shrink from the new vistas of faith
that will be set before us this day and always.
We ask this through Christ and the Holy Spirit,
with you, One God, forever and ever.

Amen.

Praise God from the mountains!
Praise God from the cliffs!
Praise God, all you angels!
Praise God, all you hosts!
Praise God, sun and moon!
Praise God, shining stars!
Praise God, highest heavens
and the waters above heaven's height!
Let everything give praise to God,
who commanded and created all!
God established creation forever,
gave laws that shall never pass away.
Praise God, nations and peoples,
women and men, children and elders alike.
God's majesty is above earth and heaven.
God has raised up a faithful people.
Let the praise of God be on our lips
from the children of Israel,
the people God has drawn close.

(Psalm 148)

Silence

Daylight has broken upon us, and the praise of God
breaks from our heart and lips. This day we praise God
for the surprising challenges that can further the cause
of justice and peace. Filled with wonder at the invitations God gives us, we present our needs and intentions
to the God who hears our prayers . . .

The Lord's Prayer

Canticle

Offering

Closing

EVENING PRAYER

Presence

As nighttime covers our small part of the world, we call to mind the events of this day. We are grateful for the many opportunities that God has given us in which to be deepened as a people of faith, a people born in Christ. In thanksgiving, we offer our thanks for the challenges we have met today with grace and wisdom.

Prayer

O God, on that night before Jesus suffered for us,
Christ gathered those first disciples at a table of unity.
There Jesus took up the customary bread of friendship.
Bread was blessed, broken, and shared
      by all those present.
And in that sharing they heard new words,
      new possibilities:
"Take and eat. This is my body to be given up for you."
Likewise at the end of the meal,
Jesus took the customary cup of blessing.
Cup blessed and shared. Cup given new depth and color.
"Take and drink. This is the cup of my blood
to be poured out for the salvation of the many."
This night we are filled with deep thanksgiving
for the presence of Jesus in our midst
who takes the bread of our life and the wine of our spirit
and offers us new insights and new horizons of faith.
This day we have met the challenges of Gospel-living.
Not perfectly but with eager hearts
we have tried to do your will
and bring your peace and justice to our world.
Make us always grateful
and give us courage to meet your invitations of grace.
We ask this through Christ and the Holy Spirit,
with you, One God, forever and ever.
Amen.

I myself am the bread of life.
Let me solemnly assure you,
if you do not eat my flesh,
if you do not drink my blood,
you will have no life within you.
If you find nourishment in my flesh,
if your thirst is relieved by my blood,
you will have eternal life,
and I will raise you up on the last day.
For my flesh is food indeed.
My blood is true drink.
You who eat my flesh,
You who drink my blood,
remain in me and I in you.
Yes, I myself am the bread of life!

(John 6:53–56)

Silence

God of mystery and surprises, tonight we recall how
Jesus was handed over for us. We are filled with gratitude for your gift of the Spirit, who allowed us to meet
the challenges of Gospel-living this day. We are
grateful for each way the Spirit did not let our fears
hand us over to doubt and despair. Thankful for the
many ways you call us to a deeper and more lively
living of the word, we offer you our special needs and
intentions . . .

The Lord's Prayer

Canticle

Offering

Closing

Fourth Friday:
For the Gifts
of Mercy and Compassion

MORNING PRAYER

Presence

This is the day of salvation, the day when we remember with wonder how we were brought to new life through Jesus. As we rise from sleep, we are painfully aware of our own need for mercy and compassion. We praise God this day for the many ways we have come to know the gifts of kindness and gentleness as healing for our wounded heart.

Prayer

O God of tender mercies,
when Jesus was lifted up from the earth
you drew every wounded heart to yourself.
Though you have called us in Christ
to be instruments of your justice and peace,
we ourselves need your compassion and loving mercy.
Fears and doubts invade our mind and heart.
Our lack of love for ourselves keeps us afraid.
Yet each day you send us the gift of healing
that we need so much.
On this day of our salvation,
we give you the gift of our sincere praise.
You are mercy and compassion for our hearts.
And these gifts you give to us in earthly loves,
in the success of our labors,
and in the quiet and dazzling beauty of creation.
Help us to sing your praise for what your love does
    in our midst.
We ask this through Christ and the Holy Spirit,
with you, One God, forever and ever.
Amen.

Sing to God a new song!
Sing a song of praise from all believers.
Let Israel rejoice in the presence of all mercy.
Let earth's children give praise
to the God of all compassion.
Let us praise the glorious and tender name of God.
Let us sing to God with harmony of heart.
Let us dance before the God who has saved us.
For God loves us passionately
and showers us with abundant mercy.
God has raised up a people once held in exile
and lavishes pure compassion upon us.
Wake from your slumber!
Brush away sleep!
Open your eyes!
Attend to the glory of God all around you.
Let the high praises of God ring out.
For God has heard our cries for justice
and has ransomed us in peace.

(Psalm 149)

Canticle

Silence

Remembrance of Christ's life, death, and resurrection
compels us to give loud praise to the God who looks on
us in our every need. Our Creator does not withhold
kindness and compassion from us. Filled with wonder at
the mercy of God in our life, we offer our needs and
intentions . . .

Offering

The Lord's Prayer

Closing

**EVENING
PRAYER**

Presence

At this hour, Jesus was taken from the cross to rest in the tomb. As we come to the end of our daily labors, let us give thanks for the many gifts of salvation that have been ours. This night we are especially grateful for the varied ways that God's mercy and compassion have filled our hearts and given us new hope.

Prayer

O God, you never abandon the poor and the suffering.
Though often we are tempted to judge you as silent,
you stand close to people whose hearts are broken.
Those who labor constantly in your vineyard
and faithfully proclaim your word
are themselves in need of your mercy and compassion.
You do not withhold your gifts from your beloved.
You do not allow us to suffer the corruption of despair,
but you feed and clothe us with dignity
and raise our broken spirits.
This night we are filled with the spirit of thanksgiving.
The sweat of our labors and the bleeding of our doubts
make us needy for your gift of consolation.
Each night you give us the refreshment of sleep
and you guard us as the apple of your eye.
Open our eyes to the gifts of your mercy
        and compassion
that soothe and heal our wounded heart.
This night we offer you thanksgiving.
Keep us always grateful that we may announce
to a people yet to be born: "God saves!"
We ask this through Christ and the Holy Spirit,
with you, One God, forever and ever.
Amen.

I myself am the bread of life.
God has sent me into the world to give the gift of life.
Just as I draw my life from God,
so you who would feed on me
shall draw your life from me.
This is the living bread, the bread of life,
that has come down from the heavens.
Unlike your ancestors who ate and died,
if you feed on this bread,
you shall live forever.
It is the Spirit of God that gives true life.
The spirit of this world,
a spirit in rebellion against God,
can give nothing.
My words are both spirit and life.
No one can come to hear my words
unless they are drawn by God.
I myself am the bread of life.

(John 6:57–65)

Silence

Canticle

Loving God, at this evening hour we offer our thanksgiving for the mercy and compassion you give to
strengthen and console us. We are a needy people, but
you do not abandon us. Instead, you embrace us in our
every need. Grateful for your unfailing presence, we
offer you our needs and intentions . . .

Offering

The Lord's Prayer

Closing

Fourth Saturday:
For the Gift of Faith-filled Joy

Presence

We awake to God, filled with joy for having passed the night safely and for being offered another dawn. Praise to God for the gift of delight that moves us to sing of God's goodness. Joy itself is the gift of God. In this spirit of wonder, we offer God praise for this new day and the new graces that will be ours.

Prayer

O God,
you created our changeable spirits
with the varied moods
that give color and shape to our life.
As disciples of Jesus,
you have called us to a life of happiness and peace,
a life of wonder, joy, and delight.
Jesus knew the wine of happiness
and the nourishment of family and friends.
Praise to you for the joy
that sustains us in our troubled times
and brings us to celebrate your victory of salvation.
Do not let our heart be long disturbed
by doubts and depression.
Rather, let us meet our every trial
with that joy that strengthens our resolve
     for your peace.
All praise to you, God of joy, this day and forever!
We ask this through Christ and the Holy Spirit,
with you, One God, forever and ever.
Amen.

Canticle

Praise God in all holy dwellings!
Praise God in our midst!
Praise God for mighty deeds!
Praise God for the grandeur of the heavens!
Praise God with the blast of trumpets!
Praise God with strings and harp!
Praise God with bells and dancing!
Praise God with strings and pipes!
Praise God with the clashing of cymbals!
Praise God with the clanging of cymbals!
Praise God with wonder and delight!
Praise God with laughter and singing!
Let everything that lives and draws breath,
Let all things that live over the earth,
Let all things that live on the earth,
Let all things that live within the earth,
Let everything that has breath and life,
Give praise to God who has given us life!

(Psalm 150)

Silence

Offering

As we begin another day, we are conscious that our
hearts are always hungry for laughter and joy. Without
joy, our life could easily succumb to pain and suffering.
Laughter helps us to stand up to trials of every kind.
Today we give God praise for the presence of the spirit
of joy among us. Strengthened by this spirit, we offer
our needs and intentions . . .

Closing

The Lord's Prayer

EVENING PRAYER

Presence

The end of another day. Another week of grace. We rightly wonder at the events that have come our way, and we wonder how we survived the more difficult moments. We thank God for the flashes of joy that helped us meet the challenges of living with integrity.

Prayer

O God, you invite us to delight
in our life in Christ.
Even our weaknesses can bring us laughter
and the uneven paths can make us smile
because along the way
your arms will wrap us in a welcoming embrace.
Jesus knew the laughter of children,
the joy of weddings and feasting.
Even in the memory of the cross,
a spirit of joy is breathed upon us
for the wonder of salvation gained there.
As night covers the earth,
we come before you with a thankful heart
for the gift of faith-filled joy
that often makes its appearance when we most need it.
The labors of this life tax our hope and faith.
Our hearts need the nourishment of delight
    to remain steadfast.
And so you feed us with these gifts
and ask that we join our laughter to our prayers
in singing you a song of thanksgiving.
Guide us to gratitude for your life-giving gifts.
We ask this through Christ and the Holy Spirit,
with you, One God, forever and ever.
Amen.

Canticle

Blessed be the God of Israel
who has visited us and set us free!
God has given to us a savior,
born of the house of David the servant.
God's promise, faithful and true,
was to save us from every enemy.
God promised us mercy
in the memory of the covenant of peace.
God swore an oath to Abraham and Sarah:
to set us free from slavery,
to sing our liberty with joy
all the days of our life.
You, my child, are the prophet of the most high God.
You shall go before God to prepare a way,
to give our people knowledge of salvation
    and forgiveness of sins.
In the tender mercy of God for our world,
there will yet come a wondrous new dawn.
God will shine on us and destroy death
and guide our feet into justice and peace.

(Luke 1:68 ff.)

Silence

Offering

O God, in every age you give us all that we need and
move us to share your gifts with one another. As the
shadows of night deepen, we come before you grateful
for the joy that lightens our work and prompts us to
sing your praise. Grateful for the happiness of salvation,
we offer you our special needs and intentions . . .

Closing

The Lord's Prayer

"Ed Gabriele's prayers are refreshing, just what I needed in the midst of a hectic time of juggling exams, children, and work. I enthusiastically recommend this book to all who seek to renew their spiritual lives through the daily discipline of focused prayer." **Christine Anderson,** mother, graduate student, Wesley Theological Seminary